Alaska Sea Escapes

by Wilma Williams

ISBN: 1-890692-00-X

Wizard Works, P.O. Box 1125, Homer, AK 99603

This book is dedicated to the fishermen in my life. First, to my father, Tom Shelford, the first fisherman I knew. I loved his fishing stories and his definite instructions about the way things should be done on the boat: "Always wait for the weather. Always put the tools back in the exact place they belong. By not doing either one of these things, it could mean your very life."

To my brother, Lee Shelford, who not only went to sea at the age of nine with our father, but has also taken his three sons and a son-in-law to sea. It has been his life and now it is theirs.

To the wives who wait. Who experience anxiety every time Peggy's weather report warns of 60-knot winds and 30-foot seas and wait for the return of their loved ones.

And last, but definitely not least, to the fishermen I grew to know who stored their boats at Coffee Point in Bristol Bay. They are a salty lot and truly gentlemen of the sea.

To those of you who shared your stories with me and patiently read what I had written, correcting any statements that were incorrect in order to have as realistic a verbal picture as possible, I express my appreciation.

Table of Contents

Preface

This is a collection of stories of the adventures of men and women who spend their lives going down to the sea in ships. The stories are told and retold when a group of seafarers sit around visiting. They usually start, "That reminds me of the time I was...." Sometimes the stories change a bit with time, but the basic facts are always there.

There are amusing tales, like when a man took his son out on a boating trip to teach him the finer points of safety. "Don't be afraid to check everything twice, like I do. Do you understand that? It is very important." Then, turning his attention to the boat, he said, "I guess we'll anchor up here. Go ahead and throw the anchor over." The son did exactly as he was told. The line uncoiled quickly as the anchor sped toward the sea floor, followed immediately by the anchor line that was not fastened to the boat.

There was the man who, after a few beers with the boys, went back to his boat, chatting happily which his crewman. He started down the ladder still talking. From above, the deckhand tried to get his attention, but the ladder descender talked on until he discovered on his own he had gone past the boat and was in the water up to his arm pits.

Then there was the fisherman who always took his cat to sea with him. The cat made himself at home sleeping near the engine, where it was warm. Then the fisherman got a new engine with an electronic throttle. He couldn't get the throttle to work right. Finally, in desperation, he attached two strings to the throttle that would do the job until he could get to town and have it fixed. As he approached the float, he pulled the string to slow the boat down. The cat saw the strings wiggle and pounced on them, causing the engine to go full speed. Instead of going to the float, he went through the float. Ooops.

These stories are usually told by someone else, while the main character stands by with a sheepish grin. But the stories gathered in this book are often related by the ones who experienced them, with a sense of wonder that they are still around to tell them. I hope you will enjoy them.

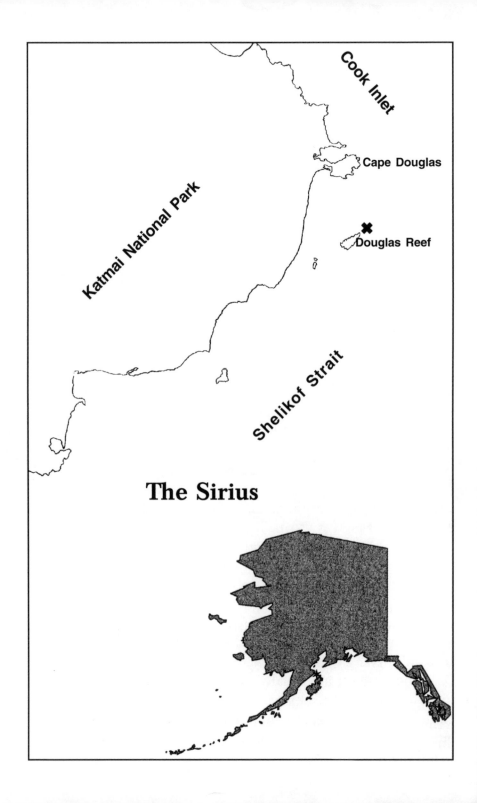

Cook Inlet

Cape Douglas

✖
Douglas Reef

Katmai National Park

Shelikof Strait

The Sirius

Disaster on Douglas Reef

An earsplitting screech pierced the black, windy, February night. Crew members of the 86-foot crabber *Sirius* leaped from their bunks to see what had caused the boat to come to such a sudden stop and make all of the noise. It took only moments to determine they were hard aground on Douglas Reef; a nasty group of rocks that jutted up out of the waters of Shelikof Strait some six miles south of Cape Douglas.

Kachemak Bay had been quite calm six hours earlier, on the afternoon of February 28, 1979, when Captain Ron Berglund and crew headed out of Homer for Cape Douglas to pick their king crab pots.

The crew consisted of the cook, Sharon Shears, engineer Michael Orth, and deck hands Fred Thompson and Jack Prince. On this particular trip there was also a visitor aboard, Bruce Geiger, a friend of Jack Prince visiting from the "States."

He wanted to see what winter fishing in Alaska was like and, as it turned out, he got more of an illustration than he had bargained for.

At the time they hit the reef, the wind was gusting northeast 40 knots. Ron thought he would be able to get off of the reef when the tide lifted the boat some. However, he felt it wise to notify the Coast Guard of the situation.

"Com Sta Kodiak, Com Sta Kodiak," he called the communication station in Kodiak on his single-sideband radio. "This is the *Sirius.*"

When the coast guard answered, Ron advised them of his problem.

"We are hard aground on Douglas Reef. We are not in any immediate danger and I think we will be able to get off on our own when the tide starts back in."

"Well, we hope you are right about that, as we have three other rescues going on right now and it will be awhile before we can get to you."

Ron took a deep breath. It made him just a little nervous knowing that if conditions worsened they would have to wait in line for assistance. He prayed that the tough old *Sirius* would hang together until they could get off or get help. During the next hour, the crew all worked calmly together, preparing for the worst and hoping for the best. They got out the old raft and tried to inflate it. That proved futile. It would not hold air. Ron talked to several other skippers on the radio.

Tracy Jones, aboard the *Sea Wife,* answered Ron's call. "I am about an hour away," Tracy said.

"I should be off of here as soon as I have water, but it is nice to know you are close," Ron told Tracy.

"I'll just come over where you are and hang around till you do get off. This wind may give you trouble when the tide does start back in," Tracy answered , changing his course and increasing his speed.

By the time Tracy arrived on the scene, the wind had picked up quite a bit and the depth of the water made it apparent that the *Sea Wife* could not come closer than approximately

150 yards. However, it was a comfort to the crew of the *Sirius* to know help was nearby. While awaiting the tide, Tracy and Ron discussed conditions with other skippers, going over details if they did have to abandon ship.

In the galley, Sharon Shears cleaned and polished. She wanted to be sure she had done her job well in any event. At the risk of looking a bit pessimistic, she gathered together a few of her important possessions.

Ron went over the details in his mind again of the possibility of having to abandon ship. He took a length of line and attached a buoy. About ten feet from the buoy, he made a loop. He followed this pattern until there was a loop for each person on board. This way they would all be together if they did have to abandon ship, which was looking more and more like a reality.

Their hopes of a simple exit from their rocky perch were dashed as they listened fearfully to the roar of the approaching waves.

Around 10 p.m., the water reached its helpless prey and attacked with a fury, lifting it one second and then dropping it mercilessly. The battered ship began to take on water, making it increasingly obvious what the end would be. Ron called the Coast Guard, advising them to put them on their list, as they would need help.

"Com Sta Kodiak, this is the *Sirius*. We are going to need assistance," Ron said in what he hoped was a calm voice. "We are taking on water. We are all in our survival gear. The boat is not breaking up yet, but is taking a bad beating."

The Coast Guard came back to say, " We will dispatch a C-130 plane and helicopters from both Anchorage and Kodiak as soon as they are available."

"That's a roger. We will be standing by as long as possible. I don't know how long we will have radio contact, as things are beginning to get wet. This is the *Sirius,* off and clear."

The fiberglass hull was no match for the crashing waves that slammed it again and again against the treacherous rocks. The crew were on deck now, clinging tenaciously to whatever they could get a grip on, as each time the boat was dashed against the rocks they were flung about. The lights on the boat went out and at last the radio was totally quiet. Each breaking wave doused the crew with its icy spray.

Shortly after midnight, the 179-foot crabber *Polar Shell* came on the scene. It was able to come 50 yards closer than the *Sea Wife*. The crew on the *Sirius* had been forced to the stern of the boat, when the bow sank beneath the waves as though, having fought a good fight, bowing to her impending fate.

On board the *Polar Shell,* the crew stood on deck. They had arrived in time to see the lights on the *Sirius* flicker and die. Each one mentally put themselves in the other person's position. There just had to be a way to save them.

"We need to get a line over to them, but I sure don't know how we would do that," said one of the crewmen.

Tom Morgan, a diver and crewman on the *Polar Shell,* also stared at the foaming sea.

"We *have* to get them a line," he said thoughtfully. "They can hold on to it, and we can reel them over here with the crab block." Then, turning away, he said, "I'll get my gear on and take it over."

The skipper caught his arm. "Tom, you don't have to do this," he said, knowing the danger the young diver would face.

Tom turned toward the skipper and said quietly, "I think I do. I do not have the guts to sit here and watch those five people perish without at least trying."

Tom paused for a moment on the rail. Attached to his waist was a small line that would be used to pull the bigger line over once he was aboard the other boat. He only hesitated a second. Not too long. Too much thinking could make a person downright nervous. He took a good look at the *Sirius* to get his bearing, then plunged into the frothing, angry waves.

On board the *Sirius,* no one was aware of this latest development. Each crew member braced against the next impact against the rocks, dreading to hear the sound of the hull being pulverized beneath them. They did not know that Tom Moran was valiantly fighting his way through the night in order to help them.

Tom was a strong swimmer, but he had never been in this bad a sea. He had known before he went over the side that it would be difficult, but this was even worse than he had anticipated..

There was even that moment of doubt when he thought, "Have I made a mistake? Is this just one of those impossible situations? My God, I have never seen waves this big." With a firm effort, he brushed these negative thoughts from his mind. He was tiring. He stripped off his diver weights and let them go. Now he was like a cork flying up on each wave.

"Maybe that will help," he said to himself. "Now, where is that boat?" As though in answer to his question, he was carried to the peak of a giant wave and there, a hundred feet away, was the battered *Sirius.* "Oh there it is!" he mumbled. "Gotta hurry, can't last much longer." With grave determination he gave it his all, stroking, stroking.

Aboard the *Sirius,* Fred Thompson stared into the path of light coming from the *Polar Shell.* Between jarring impacts he said, "What the heck is that? Looks like a seal." Immediately everyone was staring at the moving object.

"Seems to be coming right for us. Maybe it's a diver," someone offered. In moments they were reaching with eager hands to pull the exhausted man aboard.

Lying on the gyrating deck, he panted, "I thought for a minute there that I wasn't going to make it."

It was now the wee hours of the morning. The crew readied themselves to make their amphibious departure from the boat. The line Tom had brought was attached to the line that had been prepared with buoys and loops, and the crew began to step into their personal loops. As the first person started over the side, they suddenly heard the roar of a helicopter overhead.

Things went very quickly from then on. The basket was lowered to the small area of deck remaining above water and, two at a time, the crew was reeled upward, swinging erratically in the gale force winds, snowflakes stinging their faces. They certainly did not complain about these minor discomforts, which did not seem very important after what had been going on the last few hours.

They were about to breathe a sigh of relief, when the pilot announced, "Glad to have you aboard, but I just came from another rescue and I'm about out of fuel. We may have to set on a beach somewhere till morning." Noticing their worried looks, he added with a smile, "Look at it this way. You would still be better off than you were where you came from."

They all agreed to that statement.

It seems that in every desperate situation there always seems to be some humor, although it is usually much later before it seems funny. When Sharon, barely five-feet tall and weighing about 100 pounds soaking wet (which she was), got into her small-size survival suit she found that she did not fill half of the available space. Being a very practical young lady, she decided to take along some things to fill some of the space. She carefully selected very important things to take along. Being an avid reader, she chose a good book that she had been reading, her glasses, a flashlight. Since she smoked, she took cigarettes and a lighter. If she had to sit on some lonely beach she at least would not be bored.

The crew and Tom Moran were taken to Kodiak, without running out of gas, given warm food and made comfortable. They were told the following day that the boat had still been there in the morning, but by afternoon there was nothing. At last the *Sirius* was off of the rocks, and any crabs swimming through the boat would find that Sharon had left the galley spotless.

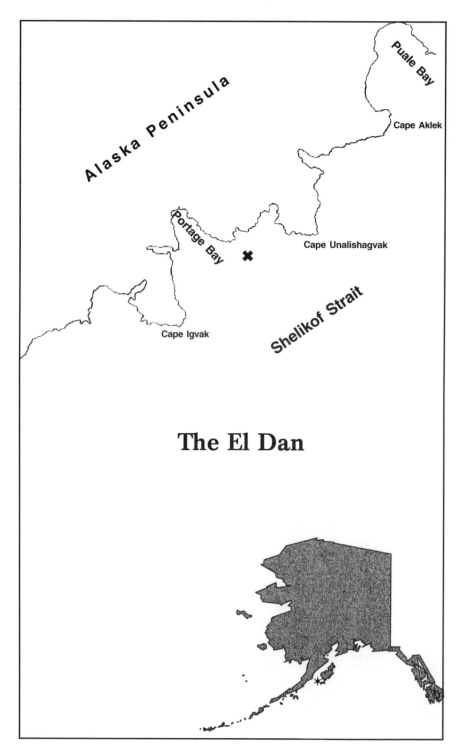

Alaska Peninsula

Puale Bay

Cape Aklek

Portage Bay

Cape Unalishagvak

Cape Igvak

Shelikof Strait

The El Dan

The Sinking of the El Dan

It was December 6, 1996. Four days had passed since the tired crew of the *El Dan* had headed home to Homer after fishing the hair crab season at St. Paul Island in the Pribilofs. The trip had not been easy. The wind howled steadily. The crew was looking forward to a little well-earned R&R.

Steadfastly, the *El Dan* plowed her way up Shelikof Strait, burying her proud bow in the mountainous waves. Just north of Wide Bay a rogue wave and icing conditions made Don Malcom, the skipper, decide it was time to look for shelter. With the wind gauge registering gusts up to 80 knots, he pulled into Portage Bay and dropped the anchor.

Rick, one of the deck hands, looked around at their location and commented, "This is getting to be a habit. Weren't we here this time last year waiting on weather?"

"Sure were. Just can't seem to get by without stopping in," Don agreed.

Jarl Gustafson, the engineer, Rick Reynolds and Spencer Allen, two of the deck hands, had worked together with skipper Don Malcom for several years. The fifth crew member, Brandon Goucher from California, was new on board this season. The salty crew jokingly dubbed him "the horn," for greenhorn.

With the anchor set, Jarl turned off the main engine to save on fuel, but left the auxiliary on to supply power for pumps, radios and lights. The night wore on, with each crewman taking his wheel watch while the off-duty members attempted to rest in their bunks up forward. I say "attempted," because when the weather is nasty, boat people may go to bed but their minds remain alert, always attuned to a strange sound or unusual movement of the boat.

Brandon was on watch in the wee hours of the morning when, suddenly, there was a loud snap. Automatically, Jarl, Rick and Spencer leaped from their bunks, knowing instinctively the anchor chain had broken. Jarl and Rick came out of opposite bunks so fast they bumped heads. Jarl ran to the engine room to start the main engine; Rick ran to alert the skipper and take the wheel. Brandon was not quite sure what was happening.

Don quickly assessed the situation. The anchor line was buoyed, so his first move was to maneuver the boat into position for the crew to pick up the buoy. Buoy on board, anchor line in the davit, the crewmen tightened up on the line. The line barely became taut when it broke again! This was trouble! No anchor, and in the midst of a howling gale.

The survival suits were taken from the box behind the wheelhouse, which was no small task in itself. The crew had to beat the ice buildup off the box in order to get it open. Once this was accomplished, they carried their suits inside the wheelhouse out of the weather to put them on.

Don checked the wind indicator. It was still blowing 60 knots in the bay with gusts going higher. Ice was building on the boat's exterior. When anyone crossed the ice-coated deck, it was necessary to crawl or risk being whisked over the side. It was even dangerous to look into the wind – the sea water droplets hit exposed skin with such force they drew blood.

After discussing the situation and facing the definite possibility of going on the rocks, the crew decided their best shot was to try to continue on to Homer. As they nosed out of Portage Bay into Shelikof Strait, the wind gauge quickly started registering 100 knot winds. They fully realized the folly of this decision.

Don tried to turn back into the bay, but even with the throttle cranked to the max he couldn't buck the force of the gale. The radar, mounted atop the wheel house, coated with ice. The screen went black. Jarl and Rick tied lines to Spence, and he went on top of the pilot house to try to clear the ice from the radar. It took but a few minutes to realize it was impossible. With the chill factor far below zero they were being blast frozen. Ice was building up fast.

The crew pulled the crab hopper and sealed the hatch.

Then, as though tired of all of the problems, the boat started a slow roll over onto its starboard side. The engine was equipped with an automatic safety device to shut down for low oil. When the boat rolled on its side the oil flowed away from the indicator, and the device shut down the main engine. It was time to ask for help.

At 9:30 AM the call went out to the Coast Guard. While Don was talking to them, the crew wrestled the life raft free from its four-inch ice covering. They kicked it, jerked it with all of their might, beat it with their fists and maybe said a little prayer. They finally won the battle and were ready to launch. Don was still in the wheelhouse, trying everything he could think of to get the boat righted.

Rick called to Don, "Come on, skipper, we have to go." Then he called to Brandon, who had both arms gripped firmly around the mast. Jarl grabbed the 406 EPIRB putting it inside his survival suit. Don was carrying the "Minny B." EPIRB when he started to get into the raft.

As they attempted to launch the raft, a fierce gust of wind flipped it upside down. This can be an impossible situation but, luckily, Rick had taken a class in Dutch Harbor that taught how to right a capsized raft, and that knowledge now came in handy. In moments they were all in the water and the life raft was righted.

This raft was like two big doughnuts with a canopy over it. The doughnuts were approximately 18 inches deep, and by the time everyone had been pulled or pushed into the raft it was filled with water but floating. As if the men didn't have enough problems, the next wave carried the lines off the deck. They crashed down on top of the raft, entangling the crew. As the crewmen tried to free themselves from the entanglement, the boat rolled and the swinging boom crashed down on the raft, bashing and bruising the occupants.

They must get free. They needed a knife. The raft had a pocket that was put there specifically to hold a knife. They searched. No knife! They had to have one. Without hesitation, Rick unzipped his suit and pulled his knife out. The icy water invaded his survival suit, shocking his body. Fastening his suit back up, he slashed away at the encumbering lines.

In minutes the last line was cut and all were aboard. Suddenly, the boat rolled away from them, sucking the raft with its weary occupants under it. Then it rolled back, crushing down on top of them. Just when they feared this would be where the story ended, the boat rolled away and they popped out, free at last. The wind whisked them away.

As they looked back at the boat that had been their home for months, the *El Dan* righted itself and sat riding the waves, giving everyone a moment of indecision. That, of course, was not a lasting situation.

The ride they took for the next hour and a half was something they would never forget. Twenty-foot seas every three seconds plunged them up and then down, while the screaming gale picked them off of one wave and slapped them against another. The raft full of water sloshed with each impact. The men could hear nothing but the violent howling wind as they bobbed about.

It was Rick who first spotted the HH-60 Coast Guard helicopter as it hovered over them. A swimmer was dropped to assist. Coast Guard policy is to drop the helper person upwind, and they did that. In this case, he had to swim against the tide and was totally exhausted when he finally reached the raft, where welcome hands pulled him aboard. One by one, the men were hoisted aboard the chopper, ending their ordeal.

As the helicopter crew served them sandwiches and milk, they were told this was by far the most difficult rescue the they had ever performed. The crew? They were just happy the story had a happy ending.

Epilogue:

When I caught up with Rick Reynolds he was in Seattle, along with Spencer Allen and Don Malcom, getting a boat called the *Olympic Monarch* ready to go fishing in Russia. Jarl Gustafson had opted to stay at home in Homer and fish. The boys thought maybe Brandon Goucher had decided that California was a safer place. The chopper crew received the Bender Award for this rescue.

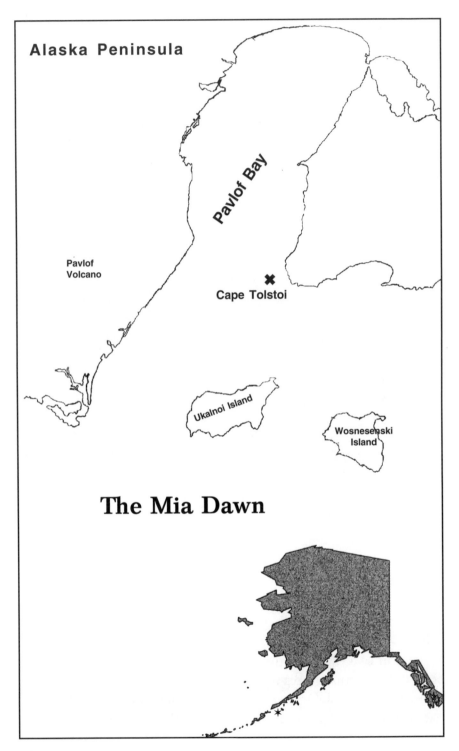

Alaska Peninsula

Pavlof Bay

Pavlof
Volcano

✖
Cape Tolstoi

Ukalnoi Island

Wosnesenski
Island

The Mia Dawn

Peril in Pavlof Bay

At 8:30 p.m. on the 23rd of February, 1984, the 58-foot *Mia Dawn* left Sweedania Point on the east side of Balboa Bay on the Aleutian Chain, with twenty six-by-six Tanner crab pots on deck. From radio reports, the fishing sounded like it was better down at Pavlof Bay, about 60 miles away. Captain John Karlsen radioed a message to his wife, Andrea, through Carol Foster, a family friend in Sand Point.

"Carol, would you mind calling Andrea and tell her I am picking up pots in Balboa Bay and moving down to Pavlof Bay?"

"Sure, John, I will be glad to. Why don't you stand by one while I give her a call."

"Roger. *Mia Dawn* standing by."

Soon a message came back.

"John, Andrea says that your depth finder needle came in, and would you like to come home and pick it up?"

John paused a moment, observing the calm waters, and

then said "Tell her, no. I have a deckload of pots and I want to get down there while the weather is nice."

"Andrea says, okay, good luck, and she will see you soon."

The wind at the time of departure was five to ten knots, northeasterly, with overcast skies. Captain John and his crew, Darryl Wilson and Jake Johansen, had no reason to expect anything other than an uneventful, business-as-usual, run into Pavlof Bay. But this was not to be.

By 2:30 p.m. on the 24th the wind had switched northwesterly and had picked up to 40 to 50 knots, causing a heavy freezing spray. Ice began building on the load of crab gear. This was a worry. When the additional weight of the ice topside outweighs the hull, a boat has a tendency to want to capsize. Captain John decided to drop anchor off Cape Tolstoi.

There would be no sleep for anyone this night. With the big swells and the abusive blasts of wind, the anchor began to drag and had to be reset. An hour later it happened again. They decided to take off the outside four crab pots on each side in order to be able to pound the ice off the hull.

John discussed his problems with other boats in the area, but his position and the weather made it impossible for them to get near enough to be of assistance. The word of his problem was picked up in Sand Point, and Carol hurried over to be with Andrea as things became more serious.

Andrea called her uncle, Bob Galovin, who was in charge of Aleutian Cold Storage in Sand Point. He was sympathetic and let her listen to the radio conversation over the telephone. Outside, the wind howled, and inside, Andrea paced the floor. She could not help the tears that persisted in running down her face. Her four children watched and worried in their own way. The three-year old twins were too young to quite figure out what was going on, but the older children knew about boats and storms.

Meanwhile, back at Cape Tolstoi the day brought no rest for the weary crew. The wind was now 80 knots with gusts up to 100. All day it howled and didn't lessen with nightfall. John had to run the engine in gear continuously to keep the swell from causing the anchor to drag.

In the wee hours of the morning of the 25th, Darrel and Jake came inside, after beating the ice off the hull for the umpteenth time. They sank down on the seats by the table, fully dressed in their insulated coveralls, and closed their eyes. It would only be a short time before they would have to chip ice again. John was on wheel watch trying hard to keep his eyes open. The many hours of anxiety, and the hypnotic effect of watching one wave after another with no sleep, were taking their toll. Slowly, John's chin sank against his chest for a second. In that second he missed gunning the engine against the pull of the sea and the anchor line snapped. Instantly, his eyes flew open. Both crew members were on their feet, knowing at once what had happened.

"Let's see if we can get some more of those pots off the deck," John shouted above the noise of the howling wind and the engine.

Darrel and Jake were out the door. A few minutes later they were back, reporting that the pots were iced down so bad that they could only get three over the side.

This was trouble! John decided to try to beach the boat at the northwest end of Coal Bay.

By 10:30 a.m., he had managed to get the boat on the beach, but with the steering problems could not hold it there. It drifted off. The heavy ice fog and blowing snow made it impossible to see. The radar was not working any more due to the icing conditions. The boat listed dangerously. This was no longer one of the little problems that come up while fishing.

"Better get that life raft down off the wheelhouse and put on your survival suits," John finally said to his crew.

On the radio they heard *Bob's Boat* say they were clocking the wind at 120 mph. The *Mia Dawn* crew managed to get four more pots off the deck. Then the boat lost its steering totally! The stern was awash, making it impossible to get into the lazarette to check what might have happened there. The *Mia Dawn* started to list to port, causing the entire frozen mound of pots to shift to that side and increasing the list to 35 degrees. Sea water began spouting up in the bathroom sink and the commode and the valves had to be closed.

"I guess it is time to get into the raft," John said. "Darrel, would you get one of those crab pot lines and we'll tie the raft to the boat so we won't drift away."

Darrel and Jake quickly put on their survival suits, but with John it proved to be a bit more of a problem. In his own words, "Putting 280 pounds of man into a suit built for a 250-pounder causes a serious problem." Jake and Darrel tried to help John get his suit on. Last of all, they pulled his hood up. He was in the suit but the tight hood felt strange. Then John realized that in the hurry to get the hood on, his ears had gotten folded over. He laughed that in the midst of such major problems he could bother to be annoyed at having his ears folded down. However, this problem was corrected much more easily than the other problems.

Once everyone was suited up, John called one of the other boats to say the boat was listing so badly that he was afraid of it rolling over and they were abandoning ship. Without delay, the other boat notified Aleutian Cold Storage in Sand Point, who immediately called the Coast Guard. With the line still tied to the boat they would not drift away from the direction finder, which might possibly bring help.

Back in Sand Point, when Andrea heard the news, it started the longest day of her life and the most frightening part of the ordeal. She could no longer hear John's voice on the radio and without knowing exactly what was going on, her imagination and fears painted terrifying pictures.

On the raft, the three huddled with their backs to the freezing winds as they soared up the mountainous waves and slid down the other side.

That morning, at the Coast Guard Base in Kodiak, Lt. Commander Jimmy Ng, his copilot Lt. Larry Cheek, Dr. Marty Neimiroff, and petty officers Mike Barnes and Chuck Allen were on a training mission in a H-3 helicopter. They had been up about an hour when they noticed an odd odor in the cabin.

They returned to base to have the situation checked. Within minutes there was a call on Lt. Cmdr. Ng's phone line saying they had a possible heart attack medical evacuation from a boat in Kaluda Bay. The crew was once again airborne.

Flying through Summit Lake Pass and on around Dangerous Cape through the stormy February day, they landed in Kaluda Bay near the boat, briefed the skipper of the boat as to the procedure they would follow, and quickly loaded their patient. With their patient safely aboard, they were Kodiak bound when Communication Station Kodiak requested a telephone patch.

"The *Mia Dawn* is sinking," said the voice from the Operations Center, "There are three men aboard and they are abandoning ship in 80-knot winds and white-out conditions."

Immediately, Lt. Cmdr. Ng stepped his aircraft's speed up to 142 knots. In Kodiak, they were met by an ambulance, discharged their patient, did a hot refuel, and loaded three hypothermia bags. In ten minutes they were airborne.

Once again, they cut through Summit Lake Pass. The weather on the east side of Kodiak Island was not too bad — winds 20 to 30 knots, visibility two to five miles in heavy rain. Somewhere near Old Harbor, the radar blinked off. This outage was reported to headquarters, and arrangements were made for repairs at Sand Point on the return trip. They flew on. Around Sitkinak, the weather improved, but this was short-lived. As they crossed Shelikof Straight the temperature dropped to zero and the winds increased to 45 knots with sleet and snow. The Loran (a navigational aid) froze up and stopped operating! The helicopter flew on at an altitude of 300 feet, with the visibility now at one-half mile, depending on the *Mia Dawn*'s direction finder to guide them. Around the Semidi Islands there was turbulence, but they elected not to fly around it due to the serious urgency of their mission. Around Metrofania Island, the turbulence was quite severe, encouraged by winds funneling out of the Alaska Peninsula passes.

As the helicopter flew over Unga Strait, they sighted what they thought at first to be a rock with waves breaking over it.

On closer inspection, they identified it as the Alaska State Research Vessel *Wolstad.* The wind was at 50 knots and seas were breaking over the vessel.

The radio operator on the H-3 asked, "Are you all right?"

"Yes," the answer came back. "We are going to the *Mia Dawn* to see if we can help." Brave men.

In Sand Point, another hour slipped by. Andrea agonized over the radio silence. To take her mind off of her worries, she decided to do something positive. She put a roast in the oven for dinner. John would be hungry when he got home.

On the raft, the men held on tight to stay with their wild bucking rubber steed.

As the helicopter came closer to the area indicated by the *Mia Dawn*'s direction finder, they turned into the wind. Flying at 150 feet above the angry sea through severe turbulence, the speed indicator read 70-90 knots, yet they seemed only to hover. Salt spray clouded the windshield. Dr. Neimeroff labored constantly, trying to keep the salt and ice off of the windshield. Suddenly, there was a break in the clouds. Below them they saw two boats. They made radio contact and found that the *Mia Dawn* was west of them.

On the turbulent sea, in the raft the three men tried hard to maintain hope, but, rising and falling with each colossal wave, staring into the ice fog and snow, it was a hard thing to do. Darrel and John had been through tough times before, and John said that at least they would all go together if that was the way it was going to be. Jake, who was new to the fishing and these partners, misunderstood and let them know if they were going over the side, he was not going with them. Even in this critical situation, John and Darrel had to laugh, assuring Jake they had no intention of giving up willingly. As if to punctuate that statement, above all the storm sounds came another sound.

"It is a helicopter and it is right over head!" Darrel said in awe.

"They can't even see us," Jake said.

"Maybe we could get back aboard and tell them, if the

radio still works," Darryl suggested, "What do you think, John? We haven't got a lot to lose."

"Good idea," John agreed.

With that, they maneuvered the small life raft to the side of the *Mia Dawn* and pulled themselves aboard. The boat was now practically lying on her side, but the radio was on the dry side of the wheelhouse and, as luck would have it, it worked. The voice went out on the airwaves and into the bouncing helicopter hanging just above them.

"This is the *Mia Dawn*, and you are right above us," John said.

Above, in the helicopter, the voice startled the crew. Every eye strained to see anything through the blowing snow, even though the boat was less than 100 feet away. The radio man was the successful one who spotted the floundering vessel, and a plan for proceeding was quickly put into play. They would use their anchor to weigh the line down in the 80- and 90-knot winds, enough to get it within reach of the stranded fishermen. Chuck Allen and Mike Barnes were in their harnesses, with the extended strap going from their backs to the rings on the ceiling of the helicopter. This kept them from being sucked out into the icy night as they maneuvered the basket to the deck below. Every member of the helicopter crew was tense as they attempted the seemingly impossible in an effort to save the men below them.

With aimed intent, Chuck let the line down from the bucking aircraft. Jimmy, at the controls, tried to defy the turbulence and poor visibility and keep the helicopter steady in one place.

As the men below stared up at the life saver bouncing above, they were horrified to see the dangling anchor catch in the rigging of the rolling boat. Chuck and Mike worked frantically with the line to free it, knowing full well what the price of this problem could be. Suddenly the line came loose.

Eager hands reached for the basket and urged their skipper to get in as he was the heaviest and they wanted to be able to help him. As his feet left the deck, the wind swung the basket with its frightened passenger wildly about. Above, Chuck and Mike struggled to keep the basket lifting upward. The lift took nearly 20 minutes till, at last, John was pulled in through the open door. Dr. Neimeroff was ready and quickly strapped John into a seat and checked him over. At the door, the second lift was underway to pick up Darrel. When the basket swung down the last time, Jake Johansen watched from the deck, ready to grasp the swinging missile. A sudden lurch of the boat sent the basket off the target, and lodged it firmly between a crab pot and the deck. Jake worked his way across the icy deck. He pulled on the basket with all of his strength, trying to keep his footing while he did so. Finally he was able to pull it loose and climbed in.

The radio operator on the helicopter sent out the message that the three men were on board. At the operations center in Kodiak there was a little sigh of relief. At the freezer plant in Sand Point, Bob smiled as he heard the good news. He turned to the telephone to call Andrea. She was laughing and crying at the same time as she thanked him for the wonderful news. She had better check the roast in the oven, as John *would* be home for dinner.

There was little conversation aboard. The men were in amazingly good condition, considering the ordeal they had been through. "This is one heck of a machine you've got here." John Karlsen said to Dr. Neimeroff. His statement was one of wonder and gratitude.

Once they were all in the H-3 and the door firmly closed against the elements, they discussed their options of getting out of the area. They had seen briefly the 500-foot solid rock bluff that lay ahead of them. They did not know what lay to the left of them, but to the right they knew they had at least a couple of miles of open airspace. Considering the velocity of the wind and the violent turbulence, this might well be the most perilous part of the journey.

The decision was made to move to the right. They would try for an easterly escape. Jimmy Ng called for full power from the H-3. Banking 50 degrees, he swung the craft into a 180-

degree turn to the east. He was able to move ahead slightly, but the turbulence was making it very difficult to climb up. Slowly, with full power on, the aircraft started to ascend. At 2,300 feet above Coal Bay, they broke out of the snow and into a world of sunshine.

Larry Cheek, the copilot, took over the controls and flew the helicopter to Sand Point, where the boat crew was met by Alaska State Troopers and taken to their homes. The exhausted H-3 crew left their aircraft there and flew home to Kodiak in the C-130 that had stayed in radio contact in the area throughout the ordeal. It had certainly been a "hard day at the office."

The following Wednesday morning, in better weather, John Karlsen and Andrea chartered a plane and flew out to see how the *Mia Dawn* had fared. There was no sign of the vessel. The only evidence left that it all had not been just a terrible nightmare were seven bright orange buoys bobbing on the calm water where the crew had dumped the pots when they were trying to lighten their load.

When I talked with Jimmy Ng while researching this story, he said, "There is one thing I would like to mention. Writers sometimes have a tendency to glamorize the pilot. I want you to know that if any one of the crew fail to do their job it can be fatal to everyone concerned and only because they all do their job well can we have happy endings to such stories."

This fact is also true about the boat: that it is everyone doing their best that brings them all back home safely.

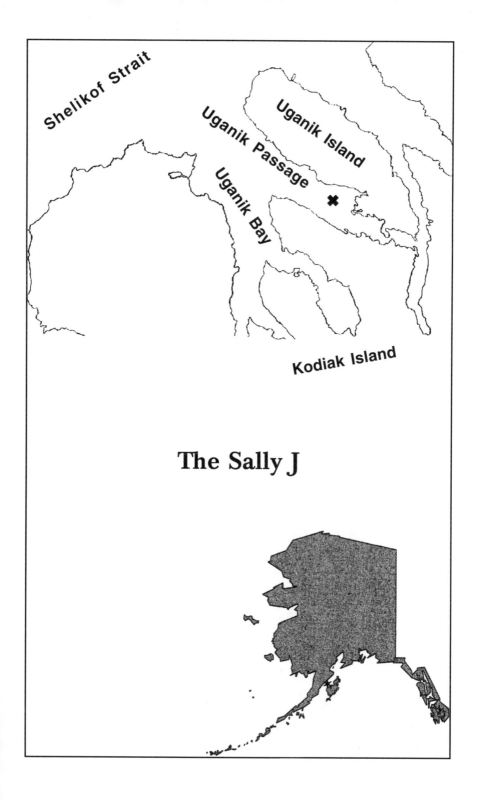

The Sally J

Fire on the Water

Nick Troxell's heart pounded as he leaped down the steps from the tophouse on the *Sally J.* He could smell smoke!

It was a calm, sunny morning in Uganik Passage, on the westerly side of Kodiak Island. Nick had just enjoyed a cup of coffee in the galley with his crew, Mark Agusto and Craig Openheim, minutes before. There had been no sign of trouble then. He had gone up topside and put the boat in gear when he first noticed the smoke.

The *Sally J* was his first boat, hard earned deck-handing on crab boats in the Bering Sea. It had been his livelihood for the past fifteen years. With time, maintaining and caring for it, the boat had become like one of the family. A very supportive member.

As he burst into the galley, his worst fears were realized. Thick smoke filled the area. Flames were coming up around the stove and the floor was hot. Nick grabbed the fire extinguisher from the galley wall, spraying it onto the flames while shouting to his crew, "Craig, Mark, we've got a fire!"

In the seconds it took for Nick to empty the fire extinguisher into the flames, he and the crew were aware it was too late to save the *Sally J.* The hungry flames gulped down the fire retardent, subsided momentarily then, like an angry monster, the fire leaped up, licking at the galley ceiling.

"Shall we get the raft?" Craig asked

"Yes, get it now," Nick said over his shoulder, as he hurried through the smoke filled galley to where the survival suits were stored. With them in hand, he turned to retrace his steps and could hardly believe the scene before him. The galley ceiling was in flames. It was a hot trip through that area and in the process he lost his eyebrows and some hair.

There simply was not time to safely use the radio to call the Coast Guard. It was 9:30 a.m. when Nick set off the EPIRB. The distress signal from the *Sally J* was picked up by the Coast Guard station in Kodiak at 9:35 a.m. The fact that the EPIRB was registered gave them Nick's home telephone number. They called and immediately put an HH60-Jayhawk in the air on a course for Uganik Bay.

As the crew of the *Sally J* rowed away from the flaming boat, Nick felt a real sense of loss. For twenty-six years he had been fishing. Fifteen of those years, the *Sally J* had been his home. He had actually spent more time on the boat than at his home in Kodiak. From January to March, he pot-fished cod. April and May he was herring fishing; summer months were spent seining salmon, and in the fall it was time to go after halibut. Now she was a flaming inferno, hissing and spouting steam as the water found its way to the hot inner parts of the boat.

The paddles dipped into the water, pulling them farther

away from the boat. Suddenly, Craig looked directly at Nick. "What is that awful smell?" he asked.

"I don't know," Nick said, reaching up to push his hair back. He was surprised to find he had a handful of crisp little fragments. He looked down at the burned hair in his hand and grinned apologetically. "I guess it's me." He put his burned hand back in the cool water to help relieve the pain.

Mark and Craig looked at him thoughtfully, knowing what a close call it had been for Nick to retrieve the survival suits.

Above the lapping sound of the oars came the drone of an airplane. The men looked up. They recognized it as one belonging to Sea Hawk Air. The pilot had noticed the column of black smoke rising and had veered off course to do a closer inspection. Coming closer, he saw the *Sally J* fully engulfed in flame. His first thoughts were, "No one could live through that inferno. Where is the crew?" He started scanning the area for signs of survivors and quickly spotted the orange life raft. The pilot had passengers but landed near the raft to check the condition of the survivors.

"I'll take these people on over to Uganik Bay and drop them off. Shouldn't take me over half an hour, then I'll come back and pick you up," the pilot told them. Before he left them, Nick made radio contact with the Coast Guard, telling them things were under control and asking for permission to leave the scene.

Half an hour later, with permission granted, the crew were air born in the Sea Hawk Air plane, headed into Kodiak.

This was not the end of the problems. The next few days were spent doing careful containment of the 800 gallons of diesel fuel that had been in the vessel's tanks. This involved absorbent blankets, containment barriers and charter flights to Uganik Passage to monitor the situation. At last, the Coast Guard was satisfied that all was well.

The remains of the *Sally J* drifted toward shore and rest in about 35 feet of water on the bottom of Uganik Passage. A sad, unexplained end for a great boat. I asked Nick if he had any idea what started the fire and he said, "No, but it had to be fuel fed to become such an uncontrollable fire."

Epilogue:

When I talked to Nick in Kodiak in April of 1998, he had decided to give up fishing for a living. Not because of the disaster but because of the changing picture of the fishing industry. He did not, however, opt to give up the sea. He had purchased a 65-foot, Hansen steel boat and converted it into a comfortable tour boat that he has named *The Spirit of Adventure* to carry passengers to Katmai National Park and other points of interest in the Kodiak area. When I checked with him as we were ready to go to press to see how the summer had gone, he said it had been rather slow as any business starting out, but he has great hopes for next year.

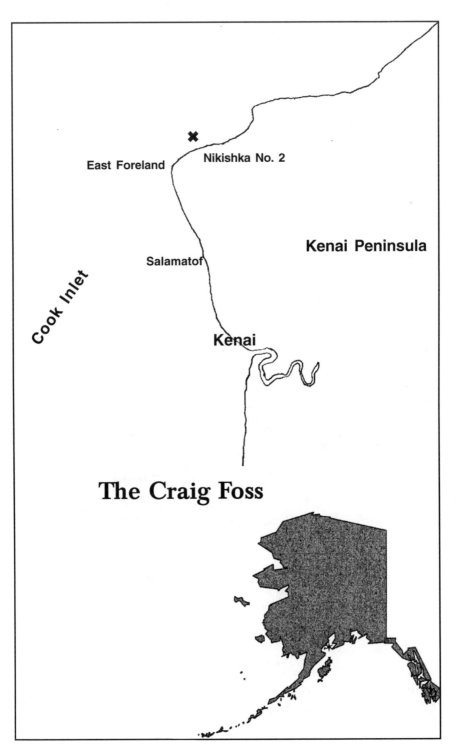

The Craig Foss

The Sinking of the Craig Foss

Through the many thousands of miles that Foss Tugs had traveled, their record for returning home safely was unblemished. The tugs went out, did their job and came home through "hell and high water" until one cold November afternoon in 1965.

It was not a wild and stormy sea crashing and tearing the tug apart, nor ice clinging to its topsides until the immense weight caused it to capsize. No, and it was not skipper error. It was just one of those quirks of fate that sent the 88-foot *Craig Foss* to the sandy bottom of Cook Inlet.

"Hi, Jack, welcome aboard," were greetings that came from the crew as Jack Absher boarded the *Craig Foss* at the Arness dock in North Kenai, Alaska, on the 5th of November. The crew remembered his good cooking from other trips.

The tug was on a contract with McDermott Co. out of Louisiana. McDermott Co. was installing a pipeline from an oil well in upper Cook Inlet to the oil refinery near the Arness dock. The tug's job was to keep the pipe layer's barge supplied with pipe. Things were set up very efficiently, with a derrick barge standing by to transfer the pipe from one barge to the other.

Everything went well the first two days Jack was aboard, and he was pretty well settled in . On November 7 things were going according to schedule. The *Craig Foss* had just towed a barge load of pipe out to be transferred aboard the pipe layer's barge. Captain Dale Gudgel started to pull his tow alongside for the procedure to take place.

Only one other place in the world has tides as big as Cook Inlet's 33 footers. That is the Bay of Fundi, with 50-footers. When that much water moves in or out of the Inlet it creates a terrific current. In this area it was running about 12 knots.

To place the barge in the right position for the derrick barge to unload it, Captain Gudgel had to keep the tug broadside in the current. At this inopportune moment the towing cable backlashed on the drum of the *Craig Foss* and caused it to go into what is known in the nautical circles as "irons," that is, uncontrollable by human hands. The current started to slowly roll the tug over. The cables on the drum screeched and moaned as it continued to tighten.

In the galley where Jack was preparing lunch, his coffee cup slid off of the cabinet, followed by a bottle of dressing. Jack's first impression was that the wake of a passing vessel had caused the problem, but the roll continued. Then he heard the captain shout, "She's goin' over. Get out! Get out!!"

Even as he heard the captain's order, Jack found himself thrown to the walkway above the engine, where he crashed against the guardrail. He heard his ribs snap, and felt a pain in his chest, then he and the railing were plunging downward, downward, until he splashed into the oily bilge water beside the still-running Atlas diesel engine. Searing pain seemed to envelop him. Then he became aware of someone shouting.

He could hear them even above the roar of the engine. It was Red Hendershot, chief mate, and second mate Jackie Davis. He looked up. They were boosting chief engineer Hugo Stall up through the door, which was now directly above their heads.

Jack knew at that moment it was "do or die." He clawed his way over the hot throbbing engine, moving as quickly as he could force himself to. Each movement brought stabbing pains as the ragged ends of the broken ribs tore at his tender insides. The engine was burning his hands, but this was no time to analyze such problems. There was no panic. The crew helped each other with quiet urgency. Jack caught his breath and gritted his teeth, trying not to scream as helping hands grasped his arms and pulled him upward. He felt someone pushing him from behind. Once on the side of the boat, he managed to reach back to give a helping hand to the emerging crewman behind him.

The terrible grinding of the tightening cable, and the gurgling of the water as it came in through the submerged areas, spurred the crew onward. The raging current worked relentlessly on the floundering tug, and now it was swinging toward the pipe-laying barge. As the crew stood on the part of the tug that was still above water, they saw the expanse of dark water shrinking and felt a surge of hope. Then with a dull thud that made them hold on to each other, the submerged wheel-house bumped against the barge beneath the swirling waters. The still dry crew looked across the six-foot divide.

"Well, it looks like it ain't goin' to get any better," shouted Hugo Stall. With that statement, he backed off as far as he could, then, running, made a flying leap. The rest of the crew stared in disbelief as he flew through the air, landing safely on the barge deck where the waiting barge crew grabbed him.

This was one of those times you dare not spend too much time analyzing the situation. Especially when minute by minute the standing area on the boat was getting smaller and smaller. The rest of the crew quickly followed suit, ignoring their bumps, bruises and burns. Once they were safely on the deck of the barge, they turned to watch the *Craig Foss* slip away beneath the water, totally helpless to stop what was happening.

The whole crew was present and accounted for. There was one more painful procedure they had to accomplish. With burned hands, broken ribs and multiple lacerations, they climbed up to the helicopter pad on the barge, where the chopper carried them to Anchorage for proper medical attention. They were met in Anchorage by a Foss Tug executive who took care of the financial arrangements and arranged for medical treatment and travel. From there it was home to loved ones.

True to the ways of men of the sea, they would all soon be looking for a berth on another boat.

The Craig Foss was never recovered. I want to express my appreciation to Jack Absher for sharing this story with me although he was visibly shaken at the memories. Also my appreciation to his daughter, Jackie Vaughn, for making me aware of the incident. Jack passed away in 1998. Also helpful in filling out details was the archivist at Foss Tug in Seattle.

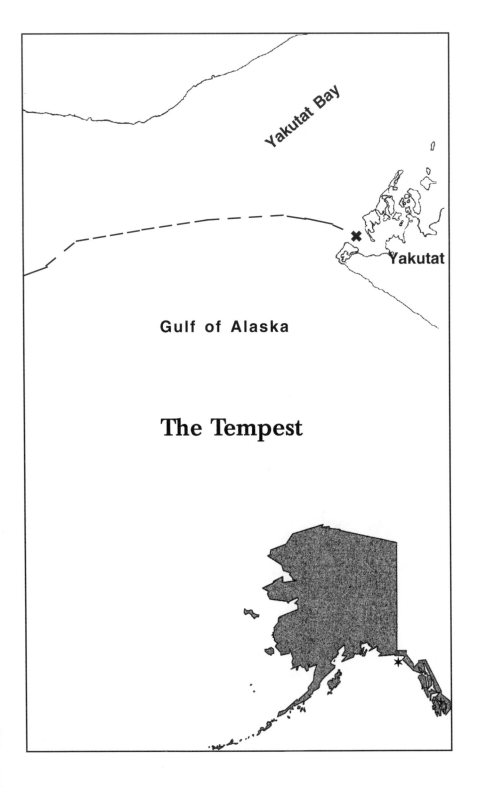

Yakutat Bay

Yakutat

Gulf of Alaska

The Tempest

The Ordeal of the Tempest

    The old crank phone on the wall rang two short rings. Lee tucked another pair of socks into the suitcase he was packing and turned to answer the persistently ringing phone.

"Hello."

"Is that you, Lee?" came the voice from the other end of the line.

"Sure is," Lee answered, not recognizing the vaguely

familiar voice.

"This is Carl Kibby."

Then Lee remembered why the voice was familiar. Carl was the one who had been running the Shell Oil executives around Cook Inlet this summer in that fast little cabin cruiser. He had talked to him on the dock when they were both waiting to fuel up. It was now October, 1946.

"Oh, hi, Carl. How are things going?"

"Just fine. I am getting the *Tempest* ready to head south. I wondered if you and Dickie would like to ride out with me. I heard you boys were going 'Outside' to diesel school."

Lee thought it over quickly. It would be fun to make the trip down the inside passage. Dickie Edens, his friend, would probably get a kick out of it, too.

"Yeah, we are going out. Sounds good to me but let me call Dickie."

"It won't cost you anything. Just take your wheel watch. Go ahead and call Dickie but get back to me this evening. I'd like to get out of here tomorrow."

That did it. Lee was on a short budget and this would be a considerable saving. The speed that boat traveled made it even more interesting. For a moment he compared it to his dad's fishing boat, which was lucky to get eight knots at full speed. This would be fun. If he could have looked ahead to what the next two weeks would hold he might have felt very differently.

"Okay. If I can get hold of Dickie, I'll call you back within the hour."

With the call to Dickie the matter was settled, and the following day they were at the boat early. They gave a hand putting the extra five gallon cans of gas, boxes of groceries, their duffles and hip boots aboard. They were on the way without further delay. The weather was clear and cold for mid October. Kachemak Bay's glassy surface glistened in the sunlight as the big Chrysler gas engine pushed the 40-foot Tempest along at a respectable eighteen knots.

Lee Shelford was 20 years old and had been on the fishing boat with his dad summers since he was nine. Dickie's father had taken him fishing for half of his 25 years. There were two others aboard – a cook, whose name has been lost through the years, let's call him Bill, and a carpenter, Irving Bagley, who was catching a ride south. They would take their wheel watch but had little actual boat experience.

Carl Kibby, the boat owner, had purchased the *Tempest* when he had a chance to take a very lucrative contract for the oil company. However, his experience was limited to the summer's project of running the boat back and forth across Cook Inlet. The *Tempest* was only a year old, Gardner design, built for speed rather than serious work, which fit this contract perfectly.

Captain Carl was on wheel watch as they rounded Gore Point and the weather began to sour. Suddenly, a loud thud brought the crew up off their seats in the galley where they had been drinking coffee.

"What was that?" Carl exclaimed as the boat started to vibrate.

"I think we hit something. It might have bent the prop to make it vibrate like that," Lee said.

"Probably a dead head," Dickie offered thoughtfully, referring to the old water soaked logs that floated just beneath the surface and were always a mariner's nightmare.

"We've got to get a look at that," Carl said. "We're still quite a ways out of Seward. Any ideas where we might go dry?" He addressed this to Lee and Dickie, as he knew they had the most knowledge of the area.

"There's a good sandy beach in Little Bay on Nuka Island," Lee said, picking up the tide book and running his finger down the page. "We still have about three hours on the outgoing tide."

"How far?" Carl asked.

"Maybe another 30 minutes," Lee said.

In spite of the choppy weather and the vibration, the ailing *Tempest* shuddered its way into Little Bay and onto the sandy beach. The sun cast its last golden rays across the water before slowly sinking below the western horizon. In the fast gathering dusk, the water shallowed out enough for Dickie and Lee to go over the side and inspect the damage.

"Wow. Whatever we hit sure bent that prop," Dickie commented, peering into the water beneath the stern.

"Yeah," Lee answered, reaching into the water to feel the still submerged propeller. "And it's going to take a sledge hammer to get that bent back into shape."

"I don't have anything like that aboard," Carl said, peering over the side from the deck.

Remembering the visits he had made to the island with his dad, Lee said, "It shouldn't be very far through to the other side of the island to Herring Pete's place." He was referring to the old timer who lived on the other side of the island with his wife.

"But it's getting dark. Do you think you could find it?" Carl asked as the boys climbed back aboard.

"I had better try. We can't bend that prop without one," Lee answered, pulling a heavier coat from his duffel bag.

"I'll go with you," Dickie offered, as he too looked for warmer clothes, put on his cap and pulled it down over his ears.

Carl was pulling out one little drawer after another. "Here it is. Take this," he said, handing Lee a weather-beaten old flashlight. "Maybe it will help."

Making the trek through the hinterlands of Nuka Island proved to be challenging. Lee and Dickie pushed aside alder branches, stumbled over logs and got hit in the face by low hanging spruce boughs. Contact with an occasional devil's club plant brought a yelp of pain.

About 20 minutes into their journey, a horrible screeching sound rent the night air. The boys froze, holding their breath. With his heart pounding, Lee cautiously beamed the flashlight this way and that, fearing what the narrow beam might reveal. Nothing here. Nothing there. He moved the beam up a good sized tree. There sat a huge screech owl, its big yellow eyes peering down at them through the dark night.

Breathing a sigh of relief, they stumbled on. Soon they could see the light shining from the cabin windows. As they got closer, Lee beamed his light toward the place where Pete always anchored the *Rolf.* No boat. Hmmm. Well, his wife would be there.

Lee knocked on the door. Inside, Herring Pete's wife heard the knock and was terrified. On Nuka Island there were no neighbors, and Pete was not home. As far as she knew there should not be another human within miles. It took 15 minutes to talk her into letting them get a sledge hammer out of the shed, and even then she stood guard with the 30.06 rifle cocked and ready for action.

Once back at the boat, they all took turns hammering away at the badly bent propeller until the damage was repaired. The sledge hammer was returned to the yet untrusting wife. While they waited for the tide to come in, Irving decided to fill the gas tank back up out of the reserve five gallon cans, just to be on the safe side.

Before midnight they were on their way, and by the time the sun peeped over the mountain tops they had traveled many miles toward Yakutat.

The weather was good through Blying Sound. There was a short chop off of Cape Hinchinbrook, but they were still making good time. Coming by Cape St. Elias, it started getting rough.

Carl was on the wheel when the full fury of the storm hit. Irving Bagley was leaning on the console in the wheelhouse talking to Carl when the first bad wave hit the boat. The others were in the galley, talking and drinking coffee. Suddenly, coffee cups soared through the air, flinging their contents onto the walls and crashing down to the floor in pieces. Irving was thrown head over heels to join the broken cups, spilled coffee and other debris on the galley floor. He got up, shook his head, and without saying a word, went below to his bunk, thinking it might be a safer place.

Carl was the first to succumb to sea sickness but he continued to pump the bilges periodically. Although he didn't feel adequate on the wheel, he tried to help. No one was aware then that he had a heart condition that was rapidly ticking away his earthly stay. Within the hour, Bill also took to his bunk, leaving Lee and Dickie to spell each other at the wheel.

Through the next hour, the fury of the storm increased. Beads of perspiration stood out on Lee's forehead when he looked out the wheelhouse window into the yawning mouth of green water coming at him, trying to swallow the brave little boat that now seemed so very small. About two hours after passing Cape St. Elias, a mountain of water slammed into the boat, tearing open the escape hatch on the bow and pouring gallons of water below decks before Dickie and Irving managed to get it secured and the bilges pumped.

Lee had just started to breathe again when another of the writhing green giants crashed against the boat hard enough that, with an agonizing scream, the bolts holding down the galley stove ripped out of the wooden floor. Lee looked back and saw the stove hit the ceiling. He shouted for Dickie and Carl, who managed to catch up with the stove and tie it down.

Lee would have liked very much to have time to be scared but it was a luxury he could not allow himself. He wanted to live. He wanted to get a chance to be 21 and the only way that could happen was if he could keep this boat on the right track. A lot of things went through his mind as he clutched the wheel and faced the 50-foot waves that were attacking. He thought of his girl friend, Dickie's sister, waiting on the other end of his journey. He thought of Carl's wife and children who would be waiting. Of Dickie, who had been his friend ever since he could remember. Seeing this through was a must. The secret to make this happen was to outlive this nightmare.

It was time! Carl called the closest Coast Guard station on his powerful old FM radio and reported the conditions. The Coast Guard answered from San Franciso, California.

"That storm you are in is affecting the whole North Pacific," came the crackling voice from the radio. "After it lays down we will try and check on everyone."

Now that was a real comfort, to know someone would look for the pieces later.

The 120-foot tug *Barbara Foss* came on the air calling the

Coast Guard. "I don't know if we are going to make it. We have taken a big tree across our bow. One of the branches is through the wheelhouse window and we are taking on water. We've stuffed pillows and blankets in around it, but every wave moves the tree around. Things don't look good."

That sounded bad. When a 120-foot sea-going tug was in trouble, what chance did the little 40-foot *Tempest* have? Lee decided he had better not think about that. Just handle it one wave at a time. All you had to do was get through the next wave.

The *Katonia*, a 60-foot boat, was in trouble and calling the Coast Guard.

Another fierce wave hit. The pressure of the waves was making the windows bulge inward. Lee prayed a silent prayer they would hold. He called to Carl to pump the bilges. At best he could figure, he was 100 miles from Yakutat. Carl and Dickie were both desperately seasick. Irving had disappeared below decks. Bill, who had not been heard from in hours, appeared in the wheel house.

"Lee, we aren't going to make it are we?" he asked in a small shaky voice.

Lee looked at the white face. Perspiration stood out on Bill's forehead, he smelled sour.

"All I can tell you is, it don't look very good, but we are going to give it a good fight."

The worried cook turned away but a few minutes later was back with a knife in hand. Pulling up his smelly T-shirt and turning his back he said, "Will you carve my name on my back so they will know who I was? I am going to jump overboard."

Lee had his hands full steering the boat, and his eyes were tired from straining to see the oncoming waves. It was important to handle this situation well. He answered in what he hoped was a calm voice. "You can't do that. If you open that wheelhouse door you will sink us."

"Well, I'm sorry about that, but I'm out of here," Bill answered, turning toward the door. Taking one hand from the wheel, Lee grabbed the back of Bill's shirt, managing to jerk him away from the door, and threw him down the stairs toward the sleeping quarters. In seconds, Bill was back up. What an inopportune time to have to indulge in physical violence, but there was no choice. Lee half turned from the wheel and planted a well aimed foot into Bill's face, kicking him hard enough to send him flying back downstairs. On the third smashing kick in the face, Bill got the idea Lee didn't want him to open the wheelhouse door and was not heard from again.

It was dark again. The clawing waves had torn everything from the top of the wheelhouse except one small persistent spotlight that clung tenaciously through all of the punishment. Then, as if they didn't have enough trouble, it started to snow with blizzard ferocity, making the visibility about zero.

The long hours of peering out into the inky blackness of the stormy night with only the beam of the one small spotlight had began to wear on Lee. Then, suddenly, everything became very clear. He could see the old familiar hill road in his hometown of Homer. It lay ahead through the night and for hours he steered down that road, carefully staying between the snow berms, with perfect confidence that he was on the right road.

When dawn came, Lee had been on the wheel without anything but a few crackers for food for 52 hours, and his knees were beginning to feel rubbery. The fuel gauges were threatening the red line. He didn't look at them anymore. Sometimes there are things you would rather not know. He was very thankful that Irving had refueled at Nuka Island.

The good news was the weather was beginning to improve. The waves were no longer breaking on top but had turned into a hellacious ground swell. The snow had subsided, and with the dawn he could see mountains in the distance. He shouted for Dickie, who climbed slowly up the steps from below.

"You look like death warmed over," Dickie observed. Lee looked at him a minute.

"Well, you don't look so pretty yourself." Lee smiled, then said, "Get that chart down and let's see if we can figure out a course for Yakutat."

When they had the course laid out, Dickie took over the wheel and Lee went to look for food and maybe a Swede stove to make a little coffee.

They counted their blessings when the entrance to Yakutat harbor came into view. The coastline had taken a severe beating. The forest of trees had been stripped from the point, leaving it clean. A boat rolled back and forth in the surf, while three people clung to it, forced to observe two less fortunate companions whose bodies lay on the sand nearby. On the bluff above, local citizens played out a winch line, trying to rescue the remaining three crew members clinging to the troubled vessel.

Lee made his way down the ladder and was surprised when a part of a sleeping bag that was showing from under a stack of boxes wiggled. He lifted the boxes off of the live sleeping bag and found Irving pinned down between more boxes with his mummy bag zipped to his chin, his arms trapped inside. He had been in this position since being thrown out of his bunk at the height of the storm. Lee pulled things off of him and unzipped the bag.

"Oh, am I glad to see you!" Irving said, struggling to sit up. He moved each arm and leg carefully as if surprised they all worked. "I have been wedged in here for about a hundred years."

Lee didn't contradict that statement at all because he knew he had been on the wheel about that long.

Dickie, who had overheard, teased. "Irv, you know it was only 98 years. You must have lost track of time."

Bill, the cook, had a couple of black eyes and his disposition was not at its best. He grumbled a little as he made more coffee and occasionally gave Lee a dirty look. Carl looked white and drawn beyond what seasickness will do to a person. As for Dickie and Lee, they had learned a brand new meaning to the word tired.

Lee brought the *Tempest* into the dock. Dickie put a line on the piling. Lee kicked the boat into reverse and the big Chrysler engine died. They were out of gas!

The rest of the trip was uneventful. They made their way south going from light to light. No radar or modern helpful devices in those days. Once they arrived in Seattle, Carl took the boat to the shipyard, where, after an in-depth survey, they reported the boat was totaled. Technically beaten to a pulp. Carl died two weeks later of a heart attack. Dickie Edens went on to fish Cook Inlet and, with his brother Brantly, run Standard Oil in Homer. Lee Shelford salmon fished in Cook Inlet, built a seafood cannery in Homer and later became a Bering Sea crab fisherman where he fished for many years. Irving and Bill have not been heard from.

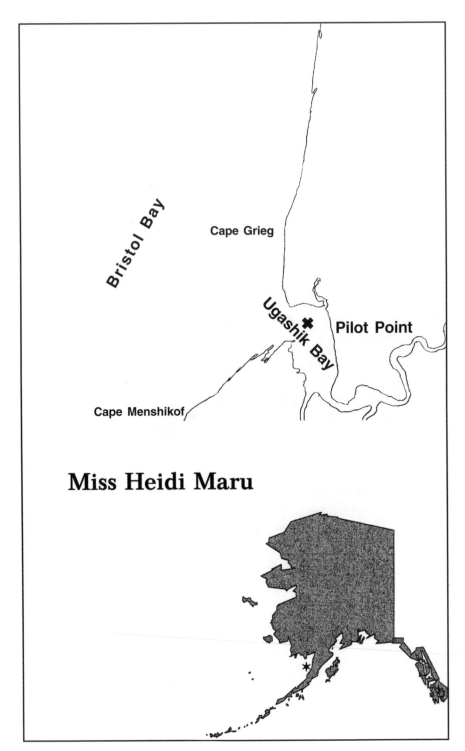

Bristol Bay

Cape Grieg

Ugashik Bay

Pilot Point

Cape Menshikof

Miss Heidi Maru

Out of Control in
Ugashik Bay

It was the early part of the Bristol Bay salmon season. The year was 1984. Skipper Tommy Maxwell settled back in his soft skipper seat with one hand on the steering wheel of his 32-foot commercial fishing boat, *Miss Heidi Maru.* He had a pretty good catch of king salmon aboard, a good boat and a fair tide. Who could ask for more? He glanced at his watch. 10:30 p.m. He should be in Ugashik Bay in another 20 minutes to unload onto the tender, *Bristol Monarch,* where she lay at anchor, awaiting the catcher boats.

A sudden thud and loss of speed brought him out of his daydream and back to reality. What had happened? He pushed the throttle ahead. The 3208 Cat engine roared, but there was no noticeable thrust of speed.

David Vargus, Tommy's deck hand, jumped out of the bunk where he had been trying to get a little rest before they got to the tender to unload.

"What's the matter?" he asked.

"It acts like we have lost the prop. I'm going to give a call and see if I can raise someone to give us a tow," Tommy answered.

For several minutes, Tommy called friends to see if someone was close by. Some were already in line to unload their catch down at the tender, while others were still picking up their gear, but no one was nearby. Just when Tommy was getting discouraged, a call came on the radio.

"I think I am pretty close to you. Can you blink your lights?" A brief pause, then, "Oh, yeah. I see you. I'll be over and give you a tow."

David took a can of pop out of the fridge and handed it to Tom and then got one for himself.

"I'm sure glad that guy heard your call. That must be him, right over there," David said, pointing to a fast approaching set of lights. "I had better get a line ready."

As they were discussing what line to use, the radio came to life.

"I've got a good tow line that we can use," the other skipper said as he approached.

The hook-up was accomplished quickly and they were underway. As Tommy and the towing skipper chatted back and forth, the lights of the *Bristol Monarch* could be seen at a distance. A strong westerly wind had sprung up, and Tommy, standing at the wheel of the *Heidi*, noticed that it was causing his boat to veer off course to the left instead of following directly behind the tow boat. He tried to call the skipper of the other boat, but he was talking on the CB and Tommy could not get through to him.

As the *Bristol Monarch* loomed larger before the hapless *Heidi*, Tommy and David shouted at the top of their lungs to try to get the other skipper's attention, but their voices were lost in the brisk night wind and roar of the diesel engine.

The towing skipper chatted on and on, keeping the CB channel blocked.

Taking stock of the situation, Tommy knew they were headed for inevitable disaster. The anchor chain holding the *Bristol Monarch* would be the first hazard. It was a taut, strong, chain, holding the 160-foot boat secure against the incoming 23-foot tide. In the last moments before all hell broke loose, Tommy and David stared helplessly at the obstacle they were approaching. Tommy had cranked the wheel on the *Heidi* hard to starboard, but without power that was futile. Colliding with the *Bristol Monarch* head-on was inevitable.

Then, like a horror movie in slow motion, the *Miss Heidi Maru* went on the left side of the tow chain, while the tow boat went on the right side of it. The nylon tow rope took the brunt of the contact! With all of the elasticity of a nylon line it stretched, throwing the bow of the *Heidi* to the right under the chain and then, as the full weight and forward thrust of the *Heidi* took its toll, it broke with a sharp crack.

The end of the line came snaking through the air toward the *Miss Heidi's* wheelhouse. Crash!!

David turned and looked at Tommy. He couldn't believe what he saw. Tommy still had a firm grip on the wheel but his face was a mask of blood. The blood dripped off of his chin, soaking the front of his shirt. Blood-smeared pieces of glass, that had been the window, lay on the wheelhouse floor. The eyes still looked ahead at the impending danger.

The *Heidi Maru*, now free of its tow line, was being sucked alongside of the *Bristol Monarch* by the hard running incoming tide with unbelievable speed. Ahead lay the line of boats tied bow to stern beside the *Monarch* to unload their catch. The *Miss Heidi* was headed right for them.

At last the towing skipper was aware of what had happened! He wheeled his boat around, speeding to the rescue. In seconds, he was between the *Miss Heidi* and the row of boats, whose decks were now lined with screaming deck hands and skippers, who were sure this boat was going to hit them. Then the tow boat was nudging the *Heidi* away from the *Bristol Monarch* and the fishing boats.

In a few minutes, Tommy and David were tied up to the *Bristol Monarch*. They took care of Tommy's cuts and got a prop put on. Unfortunately, the name of the quick thinking skipper and his boat have been lost to time.

When Tommy came into Coffee Point he had several bandages still on his face and I asked him what happened. "Oh, just one of those things that happen. Nothin' serious. Don't worry Mom."

It was not until, all of these years later, I asked David for the details that I learned the full extent of the thrills and chills of that night.

Epilogue:
David Vargus is now running a real estate office in Las Vegas and Tommy Maxwell was lost when his airplane crashed in 1987.

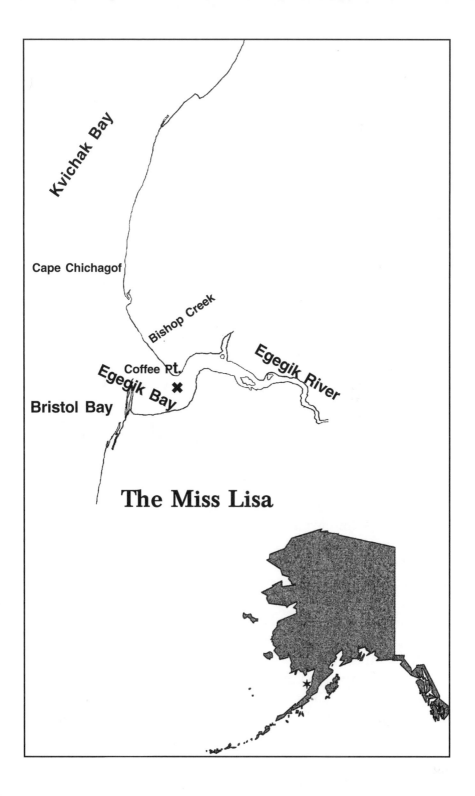

Kvichak Bay

Cape Chichagof

Bishop Creek

Egegik River

Coffee Pt.

Egegik Bay

Bristol Bay

The Miss Lisa

Double Trouble

It was a stormy, unusually dark evening in early July. The heart of the salmon run had hit in the Egegik area. The Alaska Department of Fish and Game had given a 24-hour opening to the salmon fishing fleet and, although the weather had turned nasty, most of the fishermen were still out.

Rain pelted down on the tin roof of our cabin, located near the shoreline of Egegik Bay. Wind whistled around the eves, keeping me on edge, as it always did when friends and family members rode the storm-tossed sea.

Snug in my little kitchen at Coffee Point, I listened to our battery operated CB radio while I made a fresh pot of coffee and waited for a call from my husband to say he was on the way in.

I also kept an ear out for a sputter from the small Briggs and Stratton light plant that would announce it had used its one-hour gas supply. When the sputtering started, if I ran very fast from the house down the trail to the little building that housed it, I could fill the small tank without the plant stopping. At the end of the next hour, I would have to shut down and check the oil before restarting. I took this job very seriously, because I hated that pull starter.

The CB was alive with the usual chatter:

"Hey, John, how many fish did you get on that last set?"

"Aw, just a couple of hundred, I think I've had it for tonight. What'cha think?"

"Well, I think I'll make one more set. Getting into Big Creek tonight is going to be a bitch. Maybe it'll lay down a little after awhile."

"Fat chance, but I'll make another set and wait for you."

The OK came back in the form of a click-click.

Another voice said, "Where are you, Charley?"

"Out over the bar, and it is really rough out here, Peter."

"I'll check on you on my way in."

"OK."

That would be the Most brothers, I thought.

I had just completed one of those put-the-oil-in runs and was entering the house, when I heard Eddy Duncan's voice calling from his new boat, the *Miss Lisa*. There was a "heads up" note in Eddy's voice that made me stop pulling off my Helly Hansen rain gear and move closer to the radio to listen.

"Gary, you got it on?"

"That's a roger, Eddy. How you doing?" Gary Huber answered casually.

"Not so good."

"What's the matter?" Gary's voice took on a note of concern.

"I've got about 27,000 pounds of fish on, and I don't think I am going to make it."

When this sort of message comes over the air, it is like the whole bay full of activity pauses in mid motion, alert, listening.

I knew if Eddy made a statement like that, there was trouble. He was raised in the little town of Cathlamet, Washington, on the mouth of the Columbia River, where fishing strong currents and unpredictable tide rips is an everyday activity.

Summers, since he was very young, he had fished Egegik Bay in a skiff, and this summer, with the new 32-foot *Miss Lisa*, he was in seventh heaven.

"Hang in there. Where are you?" Gary asked urgently.

I had never ceased to marvel how casual these seagoers sounded in the face of dire emergencies.

"I'm trying to follow the channel toward Bishop Creek."

"We are on the way. Just keep coming." It was Pinky, another of the Columbia River fishermen. In the background, you could hear his diesel engine roar to life.

"I'm trying. I'm still going, but the water is half way up on the wheelhouse window," Eddy answered.

To myself I thought, he doesn't sound hysterical, but how could the boat run under such circumstances?

"Blink your mast light. We'll try to spot you," Gary requested.

Suddenly, another voice filled with anxiety came on the air. "Hang in there, Eddy. I'm up the river, but I'm almost afloat. I'll be there." It was Warren Hart on the *Gambler*, and the fact that he was up the river and not floating was attested to by the sound of the prop throwing rocks against the metal hull of his boat. It sounded like a machine gun in full action.

The eyes of every fisherman hearing the message would be searching Egegik Bay, looking for the blinking mast light. I visualized Warren with a pile pole, pushing frantically, trying to get the *Gambler* afloat. In my mind's eye, I could see Gary and Pinky up on their flying bridges, engines roaring, rain pelting their young faces as they peered urgently into the night. Their camaraderie with Eddy went back to grade school days, and they would go the limit for their friend.

In her little house near the beach, Peaches, Eddy's mother, slept, blissfully unaware of her son's predicament a mile and a half away. Anchored off Egegik village, his brother, Duffy, sipped a beer and visited with friends, also unaware of what was going on.

"Peter, are you coming this way?" Charley Most's nervous voice came on the radio, calling his brother.

"Go 22, Charley." Peter had Charley change channels on the radio so as not to interfere with rescue operations in progress.

Click-click, and they were gone, but in moments, Peter was back.

"Miss Lisa, Peter here. Eddy, I think I am closer to you than the others are. I can see your mast light. If Gary or Pinky would get my brother off of the reef, I could help you here. I've been talking to Charley on the other channel, and he is in trouble."

There was a short discussion and it was agreed that they would trade rescues. Gary was reluctant, but it made sense. The unknown quantity was how long Eddy could play submarine, and when that was no longer possible, the rescue needed to be immediate. Pinky was still looking for Eddy. Up river, on Warren's last call, the pelting gravel at leased sounded juicier, so he must be getting more water.

It had been quiet for several minutes.

"Eddy, stay on that radio, so we know what is going on!" Pinky said anxiously.

"Yeah, OK," Eddy answered, apologetically. "Walt put my life jacket on me and he tied a buoy topside awhile ago, so we can find the boat later." In the background, the steady drone of the diesel faltered. "Oh-oh. Well, I guess this is it. Are you there, Peter?"

"Roger, Eddy. Right alongside."

"Right." The engine noise became constant again. "Well, I guess we can go a little farther. No, there she goes." Silence filled the wheelhouse and the airstreams above the bay. The little CB on my shelf crackled voicelessly.

A hundred or so years went by as we all leaned closer to our radios. Warren announced he was on the way, his engine cranked to the max. He certainly deserved an E for effort put forth. And then the radio came to life with what we had all been waiting for. It was Eddy's voice saying, "We are both OK." Charley called Peter to say he was all right and Gary was towing him in.

Was that the wind, or did I hear an audible sigh from the bay? I suddenly noticed I still had on my rain jacket and I was very tired. I hadn't realized how hard I had been working at getting those boys to safety.

Several days later, Eddy came by and explained the matter of running submerged. The boat was so water tight that no water came in until the breather pipes filled with water.

When the Northland pulled out with their barge that fall, the *Miss Lisa* sat atop the load to go south for repairs.

Spring came and I was back on the beach, eager for Northland to come with our freight. I went down the beach on the Honda to see if the barge was on shore yet. When I saw the barge, I just had to laugh. Up on top of the load sat the *Miss Lisa*, looking beautiful, and sticking far above the wheelhouse was the breather pipe.

So if you are ever in Bristol Bay in red salmon season and you don't see Eddy and the *Miss Lisa*, don't worry. They may be crawling safely along the bottom.

Epilogue:

I hear that Eddy has a new boat. I hope it serves him as well as the *Miss Lisa* did. The *Miss Lisa* was sold to another fisherman and still plies the waters of Bristol Bay faithfully.

St. Paul Island

Lukanin Bay

Zolotoi Bay ✖ St. Paul

Bering Sea

The Alaska Monarch

Trapped in the Ice

It was the 13th day of March, 1990. The 98-foot *Alaska Monarch* plowed her way through the icy waters of the Bering Sea on a course for St. Paul in the Pribilof Islands to deliver their load. Crab fishing had been exceptionally lucrative and the circulating pumps, aerating the tanks, were pumping on about 120,000 pounds of apelio and bairdi crab. Skipper-owner Morris Hansen and his five-man crew were anxious to get in, unload their catch and go back fishing.

If they could have foreseen what the powers that be had in mind for them, they would have been a little more apprehensive. Some of the crew felt it was not a wise decision to deliver to St.Paul Island, even if the report was ice-free harbor and more money. They felt it was too risky with the ice pack making unpredictable moves.

Morris was a no-nonsense skipper, out there to make money. He felt they would save time by delivering to the Pribilof Island Packing Company and heading back to the grounds. Morris had picked up his crew in Dutch Harbor. Chuck West, the engineer, came from Tok and had spent several prior seasons with Morris. Steve Bell, Emmett Edwards, Rick Sheldon and the cook, Tee, from Vietnam were all first-timers on the *Alaska Monarch.*

In the darkness of the early winter morning they neared St. Paul Island. Morris took the wheel, slowed the boat and studied the ice situation. He picked up the microphone and called the harbor master. There was no answer.

After calling several minutes the boat *Sun Mar Sky* emerged from the harbor entrance. Assuming the harbor was open, Morris made the turn to run on in. Immediately he saw his mistake. What lay in the radiant path of the powerful halogen deck lights brought a sick feeling to captain and crew. Three boats lay frozen solidly in the ice-packed harbor. After a vain attempt to back out, Morris resumed calling the Harbor Master. Two hours later he got an answer.

It was time to ask for assistance. A call went out to the Coast Guard. The answer was immediate.

"The closest thing we have is the *Storis* and it is 14 hours away."

Morris assured the Coast Guard he would be easy to find, as he doubted he would be going anywhere without help. The Storis headed for St. Paul. On board the *Alaska Monarch* the crew watched a movie. Although they were worried, at that time they had every reason to think it was just a delay.

Periodically a crewman checked to see that the pumps aerating the crab tanks were doing their job. Keeping the crab in good shape was a priority. Chuck checked his bilge pumps and kept alert for any unusual water seeping in from ice damage.

Night came with a few leaks developing. No chance for any thing more than occasional cat naps for Chuck, who was now becoming seriously worried. The crewman on wheel watch kept a sharp eye out for any weather changes.

The morning of March 15 found things about the same as the night before, except that enormous rolling swells moved the ice restlessly, as though it was circling for the kill.

Then the tide turned. The wind shifted to southwest, picking up velocity, compacting the ice and jamming it against the boat. Swell by swell the Monarch was pushed toward the rocky shoreline. Morris pulled open the locker and tossed the survival suits onto the deck. A moment later, before the crew could grab them, an unexpected giant, ice-loaded wave rolled over the boat's rail, sweeping the suits across the icy deck. The crew scrambled to retrieve the precious life preserving units. One short! Steve's suit was missing. Chuck tossed his suit to Steve. Steve looked at him questioningly. "Get it on," Chuck said gruffly.

The crew's anxiety had now developed into full-blown fear as they peered out across the ice pack from their small metal island. The situation was taking on an ominous atmosphere.

The *Storis* arrived on the scene, but was forced by the ice pack to stop about 1,000 feet from the trapped *Alaska Monarch*.

"They are going to try to shoot us a line," Morris told Chuck. "See if you can get hold of it."

Chuck struggled to keep his footing as he crossed the ice-glazed deck to reach the bow. He would try, but in his heart he felt it was a little late for any real benefit to come of rescue operations. The boat was moving with the tide, making it a difficult target. The line came snaking through the air, the boat rolled, the line fell into the turbulent, grinding ice. An audible groan came from the rest of the crew, who had been watching. The second line flew their way and again it fell short. Now the Coast Guardsman doing the shooting was getting a better feel for distance and drift. A little to the port side of the boat, the line soared through the air as every eye watched it, willing it toward Chuck's outstretched hands. Then he had it. They all cheered but their elation was short lived. The *Storis* crewman had thought it was another miss and let go of his end.

The *Storis* retreated to a safer spot some distance away. As the ice ground against the hull of the *Alaska Monarch*, Morris tried again and again to back up or go ahead. But Mother Nature was in control now, and Morris's futile efforts only succeeded in clogging the propellers with ice. Then one rudder broke off. A huge swell lifted the boat skyward, then dropped it with a sickening thud onto the rocky bottom, driving the second rudder post through the metal hull. A steady stream of icy water poured through the jagged opening into the engine room.

A sharp ice chunk weighing tons ripped through the hull in another area. The starboard propeller broke off with a loud clank. Chuck called out one disaster after another over the intercom as he switched on every pump available, attempting to stave off the inevitable.

When all seemed lost, the loudspeaker from the *Storis* blared out, "The chopper will be here in five minutes." On the heels of the announcement the sound of the helicopter engine overhead brought a ray of hope.

As the deck of the boat heaved on each swell, the helicopter picked up the deck hands and the cook one by one off the floundering boat, swallowing them into the belly of the hovering craft. As Steve awaited his turn in the basket he pulled off Chuck's survival suit and gave it back. Chuck quickly pulled it on over his shivering wet body.

Two more to go, Chuck and Morris. There had been no time to think of personal things while they were trying to save the boat, but now in this moment of waiting, knowing there was no more they could do, their thoughts turned to their loved ones. Chuck thought of his wife and four children. There were even a few seconds to be scared, with the boat beneath their feet being ground to pieces by ice and rocks. Ice stretched out as far as the eye could see in every direction, and the craft circling above was their only hope of being plucked from the jaws of death.

Then, in the distance, a huge swell created a traveling mountain of ice. It raced toward the helpless boat as though it feared being cheated of its prey. Morris and Chuck started toward the bow of the boat where they would be picked up. Chuck was leading the way, but when he looked back Morris had slipped on the icy deck and fallen. Chuck quickly turned back to give Morris a hand. Morris slipped again, and as Chuck reached to help him, the churning, writhing mass of ice found its target. Ice chunks swept across the deck, carrying the orange-suited men over the side of the boat into the icy water.

From their vantage point in the helicopter the rest of the crew gasped, then shouted encouragement to their friends. Sounds that were lost to the roar of the engines and the grinding ice. Onlookers on St. Paul stood on the 100 foot bluff watching the drama below, helpless to be of assistance. They held their breaths as an arm, a foot, a head would show periodically among the churning ice chunks.

Chuck felt as though he had been beaten when he finally

got his face out of the water, and then there was the basket swinging in front of him and Morris was shouting.

"Climb in, Chuck."

He somehow tumbled into the basket and in seconds the nightmare lay behind. Morris was taken from the water.

With each breaking, freezing wave weaving an icy death shroud around the dying vessel, the *Alaska Monarch* soon took on a ghostly appearance. Its last sign of life was the light atop the mast shining bravely through the darkness.

In dollars and cents it was a great loss. That was true. But when Morris looked around at his tired crew he knew the important things were safe and sound.

Ballad of the Brave Fisherman

By Wilma Williams

In the greatland of Alaska
In the year of 'sixty-two
Lived a fisherman, a brave, brave fisherman,
And many a brave deed he did do.

Now his name was Howard Carlo
And he fished the briny deep,
In the waters of Cook Inlet, icy waters,
His good family for to keep.

One sunny day in late July
On Cook Inlet's westerly side,
His nets were fishing, the fish were hitting.
On glassy waters his nets did ride.

His deck hands started pulling,
Those deep nets for to clear
But there were many fishes, many fishes
and the full load was drawing near.

Howard called upon the radio,
To the cannery miles away,
Where, oh where, is the tender, faithful tender
That will take our fish today?

Then the cannery answered sadly,
"Not today, I greatly fear,
For the tenders are busy, very busy
And they are needed here."

With sinking heart Howard heard.
Would he lose his silvery catch?
His mind raced, seeking an answer, a good answer,
How to deliver the whole batch.

Slowly, he turned his boat about.
The problem was very grave.
Could he make that 80-mile run with decks awash
This super catch to save?

He put the news upon the air,
"I'll try to bring it home."
The news traveled to his village, the fishing village
Where they hoped at last he'd come.

The hours ticked slowly by.
Howard tensly gripped the wheel
As he plied Cook Inlet's waters, murky waters
Another hour the ship's good clock did peel.

At home the people waited,
Bent low near the radio to hear,
And his tense voice came over the air waves,
"I am getting very near."

On the dock, friends and family
Strained to see the boat's proud bow
Come 'round yonder point, rocky barnacled point.
Ah, there is the *Hex* now.

Down Seldovia Bay he came,
Carefully, slowly, ever nearer.
He saw them on the dock. This was his hour,
        special hour
Now to dock it at the pier.

He turned the craft with bated breath,
To come up tide to dock.
With a flourish he put the boat in reverse. The engine
　　　surged in reverse.
Then came the awful shock.

The stern sank low beneath the waves.
The crew clasped the barnacled ladder
While the *Hex* sank at the dock, weathered,
　　　sturdy dock,
And Howard was definitely sadder.

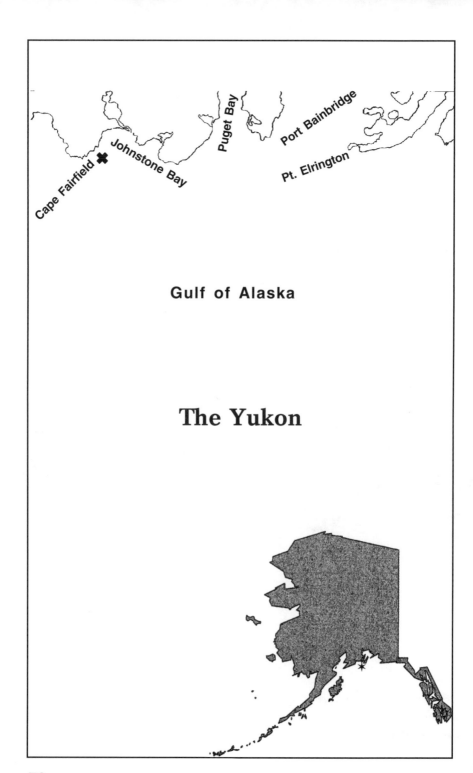

Cape Fairfield Johnstone Bay Puget Bay Port Bainbridge Pt. Elrington

Gulf of Alaska

The Yukon

SS Yukon Disaster

The 378-foot, 5,863-ton steamship Yukon was built
in 1899 in Philadelphia, Pennsylvania, and was first named the
Mexico. In 1924, the Alaska Steamship Line purchased the ship,
under the name Colon, from the Panama Railroad Company to join
its growing fleet servicing the Territory of Alaska. Shortly after the
purchase, the vessel was christened Yukon and started running between Seattle and Seward. When the United States went into World
War II in 1941, the ship was requisitioned by the War Shipping
Administration. They assigned it back to the Alaska Steamship Line
and things progressed normally, except for an occasional special assign-
ment. No doubt, the military had priority to shipping space. This was
still the case in 1946.

On Sunday afternoon, the 3rd of February, 1946, the *SS Yukon* lay at the dock in Seward, loading its 371 passengers. One hundred and seventy-five of these were military men being transferred or leaving the service. Out on the deck, the winches whined and growled as they labored, lifting the heavy pallets loaded with freight and mail for the southbound journey to Seattle. There would be several stops along the way. Aboard the ship, the crew of 124 was busy with last minute preparations. In the wheelhouse, 46-year-old Capt. Chris Trondsen, the skipper, sipped a cup of coffee and kept an eye on the general activities.

Several of the passengers stood on the dock watching the loading operation. Among them were Mr. and Mrs. Sherrin, with their five-year-old son, Michael, watching the ship's boom swing the freight aboard. "Mama look! There is our car. Flying through the air." Michael had never seen anything like this.

"It's okay, honey. I am sure they will take good care of it," his mother soothed him.

His dad patted his shoulder. "We will pick it up in Seattle and drive it to our new house in Clinton, Washington." This seemed to satisfy Michael.

Near them stood a young couple. The young man's arm encircled the young woman's shoulders affectionately. On the suitcase that sat by their feet was a large red tag with two-inch high black letters: "THE THOMAS GRIFFITHS, JUST MARRIED."

Twenty-one-year old Lars Larson, Second Engineer on the *Yukon*, ran up the gangplank then turned and waved to his sister and her husband, who were Seward residents. They had brought him to the dock. "See you next trip," he called out to them.

At 4:30 p.m., all were aboard when the lines were loosed from the dock and the journey began. Mrs. Sherrin pulled her coat around her and checked to see that Michael had on his mittens. The temperature was hovering close to freezing with a light breeze that made it seem very cold. The family stood with other passengers on deck, watching Seward fade into the distance.

Passengers settled into their staterooms as the *Yukon* made her way down Resurrection Bay. A waiter soon moved up and down the companionways, sounding the chimes announcing that dinner was being served.

The first meal aboard was always a special affair, giving everyone a chance to get acquainted with their fellow travelers or chat with old friends. The table settings on the white linen fairly sparkled beneath the dining room's soft lighting. White-jacketed waiters moved efficiently about, serving and pampering the guests. The teak walls lent a special air of grandeur to the scene.

There was nothing to indicate this would be the last meal ever served on this fine old ship.

The swells of the inside waters rocked the boat gently as it traveled down Resurrection Bay. The visibility was good. The Sherrin family walked on deck briefly before Mrs. Sherrin took Michael down to the stateroom and tucked him into bed. She topped the eventful day off with a story, and he was soon asleep.

About 9:30 p.m., the ship rounded Cape Resurrection and entered open water. A 30-knot easterly wind put the ship in the trough, and snow squalls cut the visibility to zero. Every six minutes, the steamer's deep whistle thundered out through the snowy night. The *Yukon* progressed more slowly. Seasick passengers hurried to their cabins.

Little Michael woke out of a sound sleep, desperately ill. Mr. Sherrin was among the first to get sick. Mrs. Sherrin bathed their faces with a cool cloth, but nothing helped much.

At this time, most military craft were equipped with radar; however, the *Yukon* did not have this advantage. It had only the brass-bound compass, swaying in its gimbals. The wind and snow squalls steadily increased.

By 3:30 a.m., the captain ordered a change of course that allowed the ship to make 14-mile circles. He was not sure of their location. They would travel this circle until they could pick up the navigational-aid light on Point Elrington, which the captain felt was close at hand. He really was not sure where they were. He consulted his watch. They were falling far behind schedule.

From his stateroom on the boat deck, Second Engineer Lars Larsen made his way down to the engine room. It was a few minutes before 4 a.m. Just about enough time for a cup of coffee before starting his 4-to-8 watch. Entering the engine room, Lars walked over to the coffee pot, poured himself a cup of coffee then turned to Third Engineer George Nelson, the officer he was relieving

"How are things going, George?" Lars asked .

"Aw, who knows with those crazy bell ringers up in the wheelhouse," George grumbled. "We have been going around in damn circles for the last half hour. At this rate we are never gonna get to Valdez."

Lars smiled as he took off his jacket. He was used to George's fussing.

Up in the wheelhouse, Captain Trodenson, along with several crew members, peered hard into the dark night, searching for the Cape Elrington light. Snow flakes streaked horizontally past the windows, making their task difficult. The captain checked the gauges. "Wind 35, gusting to 40 easterly. Seas about 15 to 20 feet. Temperature 31 degrees."

In the cabin, Mrs. Sherrin lay on her bunk fully dressed, alert for any sound from her son or husband. It hurt to see them so sick. For some unknown reason, she suddenly got up, reached under the bunk and got out the life preservers, placing them on the end of the bunk. She sincerely hoped never to need them, but it was comforting to know they were there.

Further down the hall, Mrs. Payne, an ex-WAC, had gone to bed in her clothes with her life jacket on the foot of her bunk, as though she had a premonition of things to come. She tossed restlessly in her bunk. Opening her eyes, she looked at her watch. The glowing hands told her it was 4:00 a.m. Who could sleep with that whistle blowing. It seemed like an awfully long time since they had left Seward dock, but actually it was only 11½ hours.

Throughout the rest of the ship, most of the passengers

slept, in spite of the rolling, tossing and whistling. In the hold, the freight and mail were tied down well in case of this kind of weather. On the bridge, someone shouted, "There's the light." Anxious to get underway, the captain rang the bell to the engine room.

In the engine room, Lars heard the bell for "ahead half" and then "full speed ahead."

He opened the steam valve as ordered and then reached for his coffee cup. It was at that moment that all hell broke loose. What happened in the next few minutes would end the 22 years the Yukon had served the Alaska Steamship Line.

There was a screeching sound, as sharp reef rocks stabbed into the guts of the ship, dealing it a death blow. It shuddered as it was wedged at full speed into the rocks. Lars stared for a second as sea water geysered up through the hull. Recovering quickly, Lars shouted to the oilers and firemen, "All out. All out." They ran for the exit to deck stairs, while Lars counted heads to be sure no one was left behind. The bell rang "full speed astern." There was no way he could get to the valves, and even if he could get there, following that order would rip the hull wide open. He and George were the last ones out of the boiler room. In minutes there was total darkness. The generator that supplied the ship's electric power was in the engine room. The water flooded it quickly.

Passengers toward the stern of the ship were awakened from a sound sleep to find water flowing down the companion-ways into their cabins. In their nightclothes, they rushed out on deck and up to the still dry forward part of the ship. In spite of the terror, there was surprising lack of hysteria. Mrs. Sherrin, having the advantage of being awake and dressed, quickly dressed her son and put his life jacket on. Then she turned and helped her sick husband get into his life jacket. In the back of her mind she couldn't help but have a passing thought about all their worldly possessions down in the hold of the ship. They had just sold the Village Bar in Anchorage and were moving to Washington. She took her son's hand, and the family moved quickly to a safer area.

Mrs. Payne was also in her clothing, but she was flung from her bunk, across the cabin into her roommate's bunk.

Mr. and Mrs. Brown with their children, 16-year-old daughter, Doreen Ryan, and little three-year-old Steven, were moving. Mr. Brown had spent many years as head supervisor of maintenance for Pacific Northern Airlines. They hurriedly left their stateroom to join the other fleeing passengers.

The Thomas Griffiths? Well this was definitely not what they had planned for their honeymoon.

In the radio room, the distress message went out on the battery powered radio. It was heard as far south as Hawaii. The message said, "*Steamship Yukon* hard aground on Cape Puget."

This did not happen to be true, but at the time the captain thought it was. The error would cause some delays in rescue operations.

As soon as the message went out, the wheels of rescue operations began to turn. The 165-foot Coast Guard cutter *Onandagua* quickly set a course for Cape Puget. Navy tug *Curb* was on the way.

In Anchorage, Lt. General Delos Emmons, commander of the Alaskan forces, sent a message to the military bases in the Aleutian Islands, alerting the B-17s equipped with powered rescue rafts. The ever faithful Red Cross began to assemble personnel and 500 survival kits that contained food, sleeping bags and warm clothing to go to Seward on the train. Some of these would be dropped to survivors on the shore when the conditions were better known. Some would stay in Seward to be distributed there.

Bob Atwood, owner of the Anchorage Daily Times, was notified and called his star reporters to charter a plane and take a first hand look at the ship to give the public an accurate description of events and conditions. The second day he went himself.

Lars was on deck near his room when he saw shivering half-dressed passengers nearby. He threw open the door of the cabin, saying, "Take whatever clothes you need." Other crewmen also gave clothing to people. Soon it was hard to tell who was crew and who were passengers.

With the first light of the gray, snowy dawn, shivering passengers stared up at the mile high bluff 50 yards away. At the base of this cliff was a very narrow strip of beach. The fifty yards might as well have been 50 miles, with the open Pacific Ocean surf pounding relentlessly against the grounded ship and breaking on the shore. Without the public address system, there was a great deal of everyone doing their own thinking.

It was time for breakfast and nothing was available. Babies and small children cried because they were hungry. From among the *Yukon* crew, came a burly Irish fireman known as Mac. Pulling off his heavy sweater to keep it dry, he dived down into the flooded galley area and emerged with cans of orange juice to still the children's hunger pangs. Shivering, he went back again. In happier times he had told stories about being a sparring partner for Jack Dempsey. Another crewman, a waiter, managed to get oranges and candy bars and distribute them among the hungry passengers.

By 9 a.m., cracks began to show midship – the first warning that the stern half of the ship was beginning to break away. Several of the soldiers who were passengers herded the people to the front part of the ship, shouting, "The ship is breaking in two. Hurry, go forward." Even with the warning, it was none too soon. The last person to make the forward move actually had to jump across the widening crack.

There were two persons on board who had been blue ticketed out of Anchorage as undesirables. They seemed to view this disaster in a different light. Risking life and limb, they went into the abandoned cabins and rifled through the passengers' luggage for valuables and whiskey.

Several of the crew tried to get one of the starboard lifeboats launched. This effort came very close to being a tragedy. As soon as the boat was swung out to be lowered, a wave crashed into it, filling it and breaking it loose from its stanchions. Filled with hundreds of gallons of water, it skidded across the slick deck, crashing against the cabin and nearly crushing one of the men. Still, they tried a second boat. Both lifeboats ended up in pieces, washed over into the sea.

On the port side of the boat, Lars and George worked at getting one of the lifeboats successfully launched. First Officer Roy Wheeler and six able-bodied seamen climbed down the swinging Jacob's ladder into the boat and tried to reach the beach to set up a 'breeches buoy'. The cross currents and bad surf caused this effort to fail and forced them back to the ship.

The *Onandagua* had arrived at Cape Puget and found no trace of the *Yukon* where it was reported to be. Upon hearing this, Seward pilot Tiny Trakowski flew out and located the *Yukon* on Cape Fairfield, 15 miles away, on the westerly side of Johnstone Bay. With the location resolved, the *Onandagua* was soon at the scene, where they launched a motorized whale boat and fought their way through heavy seas to the *Yukon*.

Some of the boat crew and several of the soldier passengers started letting the women and small children down over the side. A lifeboat from the *Yukon* was loaded and towed behind the whale boat. The chief purser, carrying $300,000 of company funds, was sent on this boat also.

The arrangement for the first rescue boats was one responsible mother to care for six children. Mrs. Brown intended that her 16-year-old daughter, Doreen, would take little three-year-old Steven and help with the other children. But when Doreen learned her parents would be staying on board, she insisted her mother take her seat, saying, "You go, Mama. Daddy and I will be along soon. Steven needs you." She then helped with others who were being loaded into the boat. Her consideration and selfless actions impressed the people around her.

Mrs. Brown sat down in the whaleboat, holding a baby, while Steven was several feet from her. She noticed his eyes were frightened and his face was turning blue. Suddenly, she realized his life jacket had become twisted in such a way that it was choking him. When she cried out, the person next to him helped correct the situation and see that the child caught his breath. Women who had thus far faced the frightening situation

84

and discomforts bravely fought hysteria as their children were taken from them and put into the boat.

Mrs. Sherrin said, "I thought my heart would break when they took my son, and I wondered if I would ever see him again."

A mother cried out when her year-old-child, who was suffering from mastoiditis, was soaked by a wave and banged against the side of the ship as he was being let down on the rope.

Just before noon, the stern half of the boat broke away with a screeching sound as the metal ripped apart. Large rivets popped out, sounding like gun fire and flying about like shrapnel. Darkness and rough seas made it impossible to make more trips. Only 71 passengers had been removed from the ship at the end of the first day.

Some thoughtful person, perhaps remembering the devastated mothers, sent a message saying the children had arrived safely in Seward and were being cared for. This was, indeed, a comfort to the worried mothers. The Coast Guard crew on the *Onandagua* had fixed bottles, changed diapers and wrapped the cold, wet, little ones in their own dry clothing and towels. In Seward, volunteers received the children with open arms, caring for them while awaiting their mothers' arrival. Little Michael asked often about his mother and once had to be brought back from where he had gone out onto the dock to find her.

It was a long night aboard the shattered remains of the *Yukon*, everyone wet, hungry and tired with no room to lie down. The morning of February 5 found the weather still impossible, with high seas and snow obscuring the visibility. The odor in the common room, where most of the passengers went for some shelter, was unbearable. Many stood outside by the rails, watching the boats and barges nearby and hoping for help. In the early afternoon, without warning, a huge wave crashed into the side of the ship where people were standing, tore out a portion of the rail and sucked 20 passengers over the side.

Mrs. Sherrin, who was standing near enough to see this spectacle, said it was like watching a horror movie in slow motion. For a moment she could see seven heads bobbing in the water. Then her eyes focused on one man as he fought valiantly for his life, pushing away floating debris and trying to reach the rocks nearby. Finally a wave threw him up on the rocks, where he tried feebly to get a grip on something, but the next wave sucked him back into the water again. Eventually, four made it to the rocks, where they clung, crying piteously for help that would be hours in coming.

The struggling swimmers not only had the wild waves to fight, but there was a foot of gummy crude oil on the surface of the water coming from the ship's ruptured tanks. Pieces of wood and debris floated up from the sunken stern, while waves tore pieces from the open end of the bow portion of the ship. This debris would fly off the top of the angry waves, making an additional hazard.

A woman clung for a moment to the railing. According to passengers' reports at the time, she looked up and saw the captain standing on the deck above, looking down at her. "Help me. Please help me," she pleaded. The captain turned away, ignoring her cries, and the woman was swept over the side.

Among the ships that had come to help were several Army and Navy power scows manned with servicemen and Seward volunteers. Army barge BSP-510 picked up ten of the people who had been swept overboard and took them to the *Onandagua,* which had better facilities to care for them. Two of the unfortunate people to be swept overboard were actually washed back aboard on the next wave. Soldiers and crewmen threw lines to two others and pulled them back aboard. An Army sergeant too weak to grab the line was rescued by Sgt. John Immel, who was on his way south for discharge. Sgt Immel tied a line to a small raft, threw it into the water, slid down a rope and paddled out to the stricken man. He managed with help from others on board to get him back on the ship. Lars did artificial respiration on him, Doreen took off her sweater and put it around him, but in spite of everyone's efforts the man died. The rest of the unlucky group were swept around the point.

The tug ST-413 managed, with the help of a Lyle gun, to get a line aboard the *Yukon*, where crew members secured it to the gun turret. The gun turret was a leftover from the war, when it was required to have guns and a complement of sailors aboard passenger ships. With the aid of the line, rafts began to remove passengers. Seeing how well this was working, several more barges got lines aboard and stepped up the rescue operations.

Being rescued was no easy thing, as the people were drenched by waves as they descended the Jacobs ladder, and the ride on the raft was a harrowing wet experience. From the barges and tugs, they were ferried to warmer quarters on the *USS Curb* and the *Onandagua,* where they were given their first warm food and dry clothing since the disaster.

At first, many of the women were too frightened to go over the side of the lurching boat. It was slowing down rescue operations. Mrs. Sherrin stepped up, listened carefully to the instructions, and let them put the line around her to let her over the side. As they let her down, waves beat her against the side of the ship. She cried out, "Let me go!" They dropped the line, and she dropped about ten feet into the raft. Anxious, helpful hands grasped her firmly, and she was in the raft. In the struggle to get her aboard, the rescuer had dropped the line that secured them to the waiting vessel. There were no oars in the boat so, leaning over the side, Mrs. Sherrin used her purse to paddle to the floating line which the men in the raft grabbed and secured to the raft.

A blind, middle-age lady followed Mrs. Sherrin. Lars remembers how well she followed instructions and her brave, trusting attitude. Two hundred people were removed in this manner before it became too rough to continue.

That afternoon, two men from the *Zalinski* managed to get on shore. Their boat was swamped in the surf, but having men on shore made it possible now to set up a breeches buoy. For the remaining passengers on the ship, hopes soared. From the gun turret on the bow of the *Yukon*, Sgt. Immel fired a small line ashore with the Lyle gun. The end of the small line was attached to a larger line, which the men pulled ashore and secured to the rocks. All they needed now was a snatch block to let the chair glide down the line from the ship to shore. Mac once again came to the rescue by swimming into the bosun's locker, in the dark belly of the ship, to retrieve the urgently needed snatch block.

The first man stepped up to make his voyage from the gun turret to the beach. Tense moments passed as the remaining passengers and crew watched as he glided away down the rope. Wild waves reached their frothy, cold fingers up for him, the cold wind swung him back and forth, stinging snow flakes buffeted his sparsely clad body, the rope sagged from his weight and he was doused into the icy water. At last, he arrived safely on the narrow beach and was met and assisted by the men there.

Lars, experienced in coiling line on fishing boats, handled the haul-back line. The next man stepped up, a little shaken by what he had seen. He looked dubiously at the arrangement. Perhaps the cracks developing in the remaining portion of the ship were what encouraged him and the rest, 100 in all, one after another, to go quickly over the side.

When there was only Lars and the captain remaining, Lars said, " Well, skipper, it is your turn." But the captain, holding to tradition, opted to be the last man off of the ship.

Lars, by this time, was in shorts and shirt. Someone on the beach shouted, "Bring that blanket," referring to the blanket covering the dead soldier. Lars got the blanket and took his trip to the beach. He was received on the beach end by welcoming hands, but he was a little disillusioned when he found they were not welcoming him but the blanket.

The captain found he was too weak to pull the breeches buoy back aboard and remained on the ship until he was rescued by raft.

Chief Duncan, from the *Onandagua,* managed to get two

rafts carrying food, water and blankets onto the beach. He helped to make fires from the oil-soaked boards and insulation, which helped some, but most of the hundred on the shore looked for shelter from the snow and wind among the rocks.

On February 6, two of the larger rescue boats arrived in Seward, carrying over 200 *Yukon* survivors. As they came off of the ship, they wore a strange combination of army, navy and civilian attire. The Red Cross was there to give them clean, dry clothing. Volunteer doctors and nurses checked them over for physical problems. Some were hospitalized for frostbite and serious lacerations.

The mail had been retrieved and arrived back in Seward on one of the power scows, along with at least one of the opportunists who had rifled the luggage.

He was wearing a woman's fur coat and had watches from his wrists to his elbows on both arms. He also had a collection of rings. His first stop was at a jewelry store, where he tried to sell the rings. The jeweler looked at one ring with special interest. He said, "Let me get my book and see what this is worth." Going to the back room, he called the police. When they arrived the jeweler said, "This ring is stolen, and this man is trying to sell it."

"How do you know this is a stolen ring?" asked the officer.

"Because I made that ring for -------," the jeweler answered. With that, Mr. Opportunist was taken away in the police car.

On the beach the morning of February 6, the 100 survivors looked seaward anxiously. Snow was falling and the seas were wild. It was a pretty discouraging sight, but out on the BSP-511, a rough, tough fisherman from Seldovia serving his army time as a private said, "Let's get goin'."

His name was Jimmy Johnson, nicknamed by his many friends "the screamin' Swede."

"You can't go in there. It's suicide," he was told.

Jimmy's answer to that was, "We ain't out here for no damn Sunday School picnic. Those guys are freezin' to death over there. I'm goin' and I'm goin' in alone if I have to." With that he grabbed up a deck axe to sever the lines.

The powers that be relented. "You don't need to do that,"they said, and untied the lines.

Several volunteers jumped aboard, saying, "We're with you, Jimmy." With a safety line attached to the *Onandagua,* Jimmy made his life saving play.

Lars remembers a ladder being put down and a hundred cold, half-starved, sparsely clad men scurrying up to safety.

After the survivors had been delivered, it was Jimmy who returned to the beach the following day, along with 12 Alaska Scouts, to search for any bodies or survivors. None were found. During the night, a snow slide had covered a good portion of the narrow beach. When friends commented on his heroic actions later, Jimmy seemed surprised and said simply, "I sure as hell hope that nobody would go off and leave me if I was on that beach freezin' my sorry butt off."

When Lars got into Seward, he was met by his worried sister and brother-in-law, who took him to their home. Now that the emergency was over, he suddenly realized that never in his 21 years had he ever been this tired. He took a shower, had a good dinner and went to bed. Eighteen hours later he awoke. There had been a phone call saying that all of the passengers and crewmen from the *Yukon* would be taken south on the *Alaska.*

On board the *Alaska,* Lars was surprised when a former *Yukon* passenger saw him and said, "I think this is your sweater. It sure saved my life." Another, hearing the conversation, said, "Oh, I have your pants down in my stateroom. I'll go get them."

Captain Trodenson lost his licence for six months and was then allowed to go to sea, never having any other sea disasters. This suspension was for having changed course.

Eleven people were lost in this sinking. It was a terrible tragedy. If it had not been for the Coast Guard ships and crews, the military barges with their volunteer crews, and the members of the *Yukon* crew who never slept or ate during the

90

grueling 72-plus hours and assisted in every way possible, the list of missing would have been much longer. The people of Seward assisted in so many different ways. Caring for the children, taking survivors in their homes, delivering the people to the homes or hospital. I am sure there are many unsung heroes whose stories have never been told. In the museum at Seward, Alaska, that brass-bound compass and a porthole are on display. All that is left of a once proud ship. The people? Well, in those days they did what they needed to and got on with their lives. They didn't know about all of this "stress" business of today.

Iliamna Lake

Flat Island

Porcupine Island

Pile Bay

Pile Bay Village

The Sand Piper

The Sand Piper's Journey

It was fall in Coffee Point on the shores of Egegik Bay. Time to store things for the winter and break camp after the fishing season. I had to get back to Homer and get the boys ready for school, which would start in a couple of weeks. My husband, Charlie Williams, had purchased a 32-foot hull that he would tow home with our boat the *Sand Piper*.

The trip would take him from the mouth of the Egegik river in Bristol Bay, up the Kvichak River, 100 miles eastward across Iliamna Lake, portage from Pile Bay 14 miles, and 70 miles across Cook Inlet to Homer in Kachemak Bay.

"How long do you think it will take?" I asked.

"Oh, I should be there in a week with everything working right," he assured me. He could never have guessed how un-right it was going to be.

"Dad, I want to go with you," our ten-year-old David pleaded.

With some reluctance, I finally agreed. Charlie assured me they would be in Homer in plenty of time for school in two weeks. David was delighted. He immediately got his duffle bag and started packing his sea-going gear for the trip.

Our fishing gear was stored away, the windows boarded up against invading bears and winter storms, and suitcases ready. That evening we kept our 7 o'clock radio schedule with Charlie's mother in Homer.

"David and Charlie will be on their way up to the lake tomorrow as soon as the tide is right. Does Dad know?" I asked. Charlie's father, who hauled the boats over the portage at Pile Bay, came on the air to say he would be listening for Charlie to contact him on the CB radio when he got close. We chatted with him briefly. Then it was time to take down the radio antennas that were our contact with the outside world and store them.

Plans went as scheduled the next morning. Seeing my worried look as I climbed into the plane to leave, Charlie said, "Don't worry. We will give you a call on the phone from Red Clark's place when we get to Naknek and we'll be home in a week."

As I flew away, I looked down at the *Sand Piper* riding at anchor, out in front of the house with the *David-Bradley* (the name we had decided on for the hull with the great future) tied off the stern. The *D-B* was loaded with things that needed to go back to Homer. Charlie and David planned to stay aboard that night and leave early the next morning.

A local family who lived year-around in the area invited them to come over and have duck soup with them that evening. Charlie and David gladly accepted. They were tired and very hungry. Duck soup sounded good. They did have a moment of indecision when the pot was put on the table and the duck still had his head and feet on. David turned pale and mumbled that what he really liked was just broth.

They slept aboard the *Sand Piper* that night. David awoke first the next morning, not being used to his bedroom doing so much moving around. The boat was really bouncing around and he quickly jumped out of his bunk to see what was going on. The wind had picked up, and he was horrified when he saw the *D-B*. It was barely visible above the water. "Dad! Dad! Come quick." They spent the next two days getting the *David-Bradley* pumped out and the freight dried out. Everything had to be repacked. At last they were ready and the weather was a little better.

In Homer, by the second day with no radio contact, I walked the floor and tried to keep my imagination from going wild. The mother-wife capability of worrying far surpasses any other mental process for the rapidity with which it gains momentum. I called Red Clark. How could they possibly take that long to make the 40 miles between Coffee Point and Naknek.

"Have you seen Charlie and David?" I asked hopefully.

"No, but I will take a walk down to the dock and see if they are tied up there."

"Oh, please do. I hate to be a bother but I need to know if they have gotten that far."

When he called me back saying there was no sign of them at the dock, I called Peninsula Airways and asked if the pilots would keep an eye out for them.

At Coffee Point, the good ship *Sand Piper* was now under way. Catching a fair tide they made good time until they were about five miles out, where they ran into rough seas. They had to turn back. Charlie decided to run into Big Creek to hold for weather.

The third day, I called Red again, which was fruitless. I called Peninsula Airways and asked them to send a plane to check Coffee Point and bill me for the trip. They called back. No sign of Charlie and David at Coffee Point. I alternated that day between trying to think of any reasonable explanation for them taking five days to make a four or five hour trip, and chartering a plane to go find them. Just about the time I was ready to do the latter, the phone rang.

"Hi Mom." It was David and they were in Naknek. Between Charlie and David I got the first chapter in the "Saga of the *Sand Piper's* Journey." The next leg of the journey would be from Naknek up the Kvichak and on down Lake Iliamna to Pile Bay.

When Charlie got on the phone, he explained his plans. "In a couple of days Jackie Drew will be taking a load of freight up to the lake on the *CB-1*. He offered to tow us up and I think I will take him up on the offer. That river is a real bear to navigate. Jackie has done it so many times he knows every bend by heart." I agreed it was a great idea.

The *CB-1* pulled out of Naknek about 10 a.m. in the morning, with the *Sand Piper* and *D-B* meekly following behind. At the last minute another friend of Jackie's also tied his boat on and the nautical caravan was under way. David was excited about riding on the power scow and spent the next several hours taking pictures and observing the changing country. By evening they were progressing up the winding Kvichak River. David followed his dad around, listening as the men swapped fishing stories, but soon the steady hum of the engines and a busy day took their toll. David crawled into a bunk and was soon sleeping soundly.

At 1:30 a.m., Jackie was on the wheel, skillfully maneuvering the barge up the winding Kvichak River. Charlie was on deck with Secallie, who was deck-handing for Jackie, when suddenly there was an abrupt jerk. One of the boats under tow had grounded. The tow line snapped across the stern, catching Secallie across the ankles and catapulting him through the air into the river.

Charlie shouted, alerting Jackie to the problem, then grabbed a flash light. The golden beam pierced the dark night, revealing Secallie trying to stand up in the water. Each time he attempted to stand, he fell back into the river. A coil of line lay on the barge deck, and Charlie threw the end of the line toward Secallie. It wiggled its way in the river current toward the wet, cold man. In minutes, Charlie and the owner of the other boat under tow pulled Secallie aboard where he immediately collapsed onto the deck. His shoe lay at an odd angle and Charlie gingerly pulled the pants cuff back to see if the ankle

96

was broken. He was shocked. Secallie's foot had been severed and was attached to his leg by only the Achilles tendon.

They placed the injured man in a bunk with the injured leg elevated. David, who was in the upper bunk, lay wide-eyed and quite frightened. He waited for the man to moan in pain, but no sound came from the lower bunk. David suddenly wondered if the man might be dead, and peaked over the side of the bunk. Secallie lay quiet and tense. He smiled a wan tired smile at the young face above him.

In the wheel house, Jackie spun the wheel of the *CB-1* turning the barge down river. Secallie needed hospital care immediately. In Jackie's other hand was his radio microphone. In a tense voice he started calling Peninsula Airways.

"Pen Air Naknek, Pen Air Naknek. Have you got it on, Georgie? This is the *CB-1* and I have an emergency. Come back." Hopefully, he turned up the volume but was rewarded by only crackling static. After he had repeated this message several times, a voice came from the radio so loud it made him jump.

"This is .... I am in Redding California," said the voice "Is there anything I can do to help?"

Gratefully, Jackie gave the man instructions to call Pen Air's number in Naknek with the message that he was coming flank speed down the Kvichak and needed a plane to meet them at Levelock to medevac Secallie. The Good Samaritan on the radio made the contact and as the *CB-1* tied up in Levelock Pen Air's Cherokee 6 soared overhead for the pickup.

With that problem taken care of, the *CB-1* again started its easterly trek up the Kvichak. The following day, with a 35-knot wind blowing, they anchored up in Igiugig, just inside of Iliamna Lake. They visited at the lodge while they waited out the storm. On the third day the weather was better, but not good. Jackie decided it was time to push on. By evening, they had anchored at New Halen. From here on the Sand Piper would be on its own.

Back in Homer, I worried. Once again there seemed to be no way that journey could take that much time. School had started, and I could just imagine David's pure joy at doing something far more exciting than studying. I kept radio schedule every evening from Homer with Charlie's father at Pile Bay, hoping for news that he was in radio contact with Charlie and David. He tried not to worry me further, but the answer to my question, "How is the weather?" always got the same answer. "Blowing!"

At long last I got the answer I had been waiting for. "I had contact with them about an hour ago. They have been held up by weather and are tired but fine. We will pull them out of the water tomorrow and take them over to the Iliamna Bay side." What a relief for them and for me.

When they were safely in Pile Bay, the weather turned sour on the Cook Inlet side. It was the last week of moose hunting season. Charlie, being back in his boyhood surroundings, with his folks, made good use of the time he spent there by going hunting each day. David followed two steps behind. On the last day of moose season they downed a big bull. Charlie dressed it out and wrapped the quarters in cheese cloth for the trip to Homer.

David was now two weeks late for school. When I heard there was a plane going to Pile Bay, I insisted he get on it and come home. Charlie would bring the boat over as soon as the weather was favorable. Then started a week-long procedure of: put the meat aboard, go out as far as the mouth of the bay, turn back, unload the meat, take it back to Pile Bay, and the next morning, do it all over again.

Finally came the time when the little 28-foot *Sand Piper*, with its tow, left Iliamna Bay and continued on the last leg of the journey. Charlie had estimated 6 or 7 hours for the trip, and his father kept the morning schedule to let me know he was underway.

In six hours I went up on the hill and searched the horizon with the binoculars. Nothing. Seven hours, nothing. When it got dark, I watched for the light and finally went aboard one of the boats in the harbor, and asked to use the radio. No answer. Twelve hours! I called on the radio again.

98

The radio sat there crackling, and then there came a tired voice.

"This is the *Sand Piper*, I am just off Yukon Island. Be there in 20 minutes."

The *Sand Piper* and Charlie were both quite a sight. During his travels, Charlie's beard had grown out. His hair was light brown, but the beard was a very definite red. The boat looked like it had been through the war. There were bear paw marks and scratches all over the bow where the bears had been able to smell the moose meat on the nights the meat had been taken back to Pile Bay. The good part was that everyone and the boats were home safe. The moose meat to see us through the winter was a bonus.

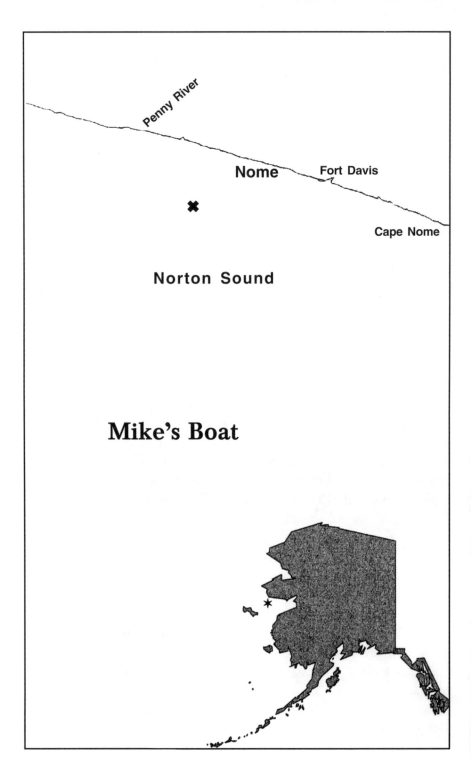

Penny River

Nome

Fort Davis

Cape Nome

Norton Sound

Mike's Boat

Out on the Ice

It was spring in Nome, Alaska. To Mike Minix and his hunting partners, that meant it was time for their annual spring hunt for the bearded seal and maybe a walrus. Not only would this be a welcome addition to their own larders, but also for the elderly members of the village with whom they would share. Mike called Danny Aukon and Carlton Tabhone, who had been a part of the hunting party for many years. Danny would bring his son, Darryl. Darryl was now nine, but he had been hunting with the men for the past two years.

The meat would be used to make their native dishes, and the hides would be made into useful things. It was part of their culture to waste nothing.

There was a flurry of activity as the food and supplies were collected for the hunt. They planned to go only for the day, but would carry gas and food enough for five days, for safety. each hunter knew from experience that dressing for the weather was vital. Warm fur parkas, bunny boots, and insulated undergarments were protection against the icy winds that could come up so quickly in this far northern environment. Rifles, knives and a harpoon were all part of the equipment. There was also a ten-foot pole with a hook on the end that was used to retrieve the seal.

At 8:30 a.m. on Sunday morning, the 26th of April, 1998, the party left Nome in Mike's 18-foot Lund skiff. They were in good spirits as the 40-horsepower outboard engine putted along, carrying them seaward.

Mike maneuvered the skiff carefully through the shore ice. This kind of hunting is not for the faint hearted. For these young men it was a way of life. As a precaution, they monitored the weather conditions hourly on the small portable radio they carried with them. This would keep them aware of the direction of the wind and its velocity. At this time of the year, a change in wind direction could cause unpredictable ice movements.

Traveling quietly amid the ice cakes in their white boat, they spotted their first seal. A good shot and they put it into the skiff. A little while later, they got a second one.

The wind was picking up, and by now they were about 20 miles offshore. On the last hourly check, the radio warned that the wind was easterly and a storm front was headed their way. Mike turned the boat toward home. The outboard motor was not functioning well, and before long it quit. Mike worked on it and got it running, but it was only a temporary reprieve. It would start and run for a few minutes, then quit again.

The chilling wind was now brisk enough to be a problem.

"I think we better pull up on the ice," Mike said. Everyone agreed, and soon they had pulled up alongside a large, flat, ice cake. The supplies were unloaded and the boat pulled onto the ice and turned on its side.

It was getting late. They were tired and decided to get some sleep. They would see how things looked in the morning. About 11:30 p.m., Mike was awakened by strange sounds. He lay there for a moment, trying to identify them. Suddenly, he realized the ice they were sleeping on was breaking up. He woke the others and they pulled everything to a more solid section of their temporary residence, then went back to sleep. It was a comfort to see the lights of Nome flickering in the distance as they trudged back and forth, rearranging their sleeping quarters.

Morning brought several developments. The wind had changed and was out of the south, compacting the ice between them and the shore, closing the open leads. They were now only about five miles from the shore.

Mike considered the options. The boat could not go through the pack ice, even if they could get the engine running. The ice they were on was still stable, but ice cakes are not at all dependable for lengthy stays. The men talked the situation over and decided to try their luck over the ice bergs to shore. They would leave everything except the seal-hook pole, the harpoon and an ice pole, called a tuk in their language, and try for shore.

During all of this ordeal, nine-year-old Darryl had braved the conditions without complaint. Each facet of the shoreward trek was done with care, climbing from one ice berg to another. Each time, they used a pole between the hunter who was jumping or going across a soft place and someone on safer ice. This precaution paid off when Mike slid into the water and was quickly pulled to safety. It wasn't long until they had each been into the water.

About two hours into their walk, they heard a helicopter. They were elated when they heard the sound. They waved their arms and shouted, thinking how wonderful it would be to be rescued, but the helicopter flew on.

They resumed their tedious journey for another four hours. At last, they were on solid ground. What a wonderful feeling. They were still approximately two and a half miles from Nome and, in spite of his strong will, Darryl was becoming exhausted. Leaving the others in a deserted cabin, Mike walked on into Nome to get help.

Worried wives welcomed them. Friends came by. It was good to be home, even if their seals, boat and other supplies floated around the Bering Sea.

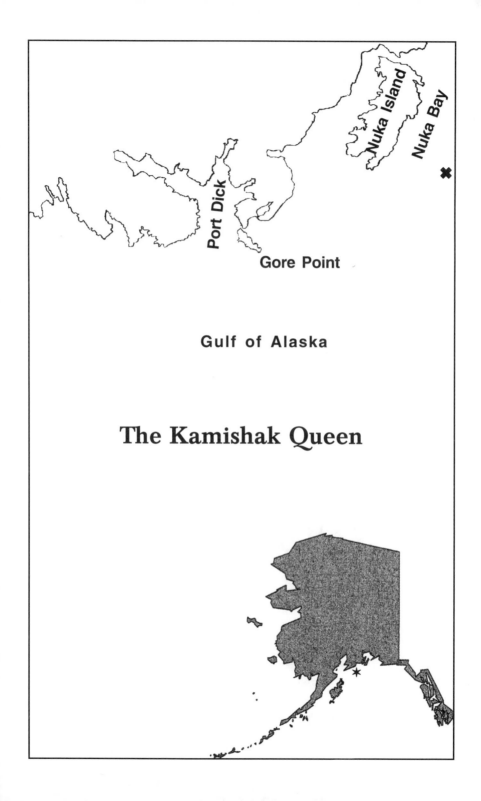

Nuka Island

Nuka Bay

Port Dick

Gore Point

Gulf of Alaska

The Kamishak Queen

A Good Boat Gone

Steve Fogg steered the 76-foot *Kamishak Queen* through the semi-darkness of the Alaska summer night. Rounding Gore Point and heading into McCarthy Pass, he glanced at his watch. He would call Charles Hagen, his fishing partner and co-owner of the boat, soon for his wheel watch. For the past seven years he and Charles had fished the *Kamishak Queen* and made a good living.

Suddenly, the howling siren of the high water alarm rent the silence. Steve jumped, in spite of the fact the alarm was inclined to go off quite often. If they used the shipboard washing machine, it went off. If the bilge needed pumping, it went off.

Charles was awake immediately. Rubbing the sleep from his eyes, he headed for the engine room saying, "I'll check it,

Steve."

There was no special urgency to his movements or voice because of the repetitious behavior of the alarm.

Opening the companion way that led to the engine room, Charles could not believe what he was seeing. Water was spraying from the center of the boat in a huge stream clear to the ceiling.

"We've got trouble," he called out to Steve as he bounded down the steps into the already waist-deep water. He tried to feel where the water was coming from, but the terrific water pressure pushed his hands away, making it impossible to feel where the problem was. From the location of the geyser, he knew it involved a three-inch foot valve and a through-hull fitting located close to the keel.

Noticing the water level was getting dangerously close to the electrical box, Charles hurried out of the water and up the steps. Steve was on the radio with the Coast Guard. Charles got the raft down and in minutes they were paddling away from the vessel.

Charles paused in his rowing and they looked back toward the boat. "When you look at it, it doesn't look like there's much wrong with it, does it?" Charles commented.

"Let's go back," Steve said. "Maybe there is something we can do to save it."

Immediately they started paddling back, using their hands and feet in the absence of oars. Eagerly, Steve hopped aboard. They heard the pumps stop. Charles started to tie the raft up as Steve opened the door to the engine room.

Leaping back into the raft, Steve shouted, "Go! She's going down!"

They paddled frantically. As though reluctant to leave without them, the *Kamishak Queen* reached out with long sucking arms, trying to pull them toward her as she sank beneath the waves. As they struggled to get away their hearts pounded, knowing that their return to the boat had been a near fatal mistake.

In the next two hours they didn't talk a lot, each busy with his own thoughts. Thinking of the changes in plans. They wouldn't be going on the grid tomorrow in Seward. There would be no tendering contract next week. They had suffered a bad financial blow. There were other things too. Would the Coast Guard find them? There was a lot of water to search over in the semi-darkness.

Then the wonderful sound of the helicopter engine came to them and soon they were in the chopper flying toward Kodiak. By the time the sun was coming up they were talking about how to go about getting another boat and get back fishing.

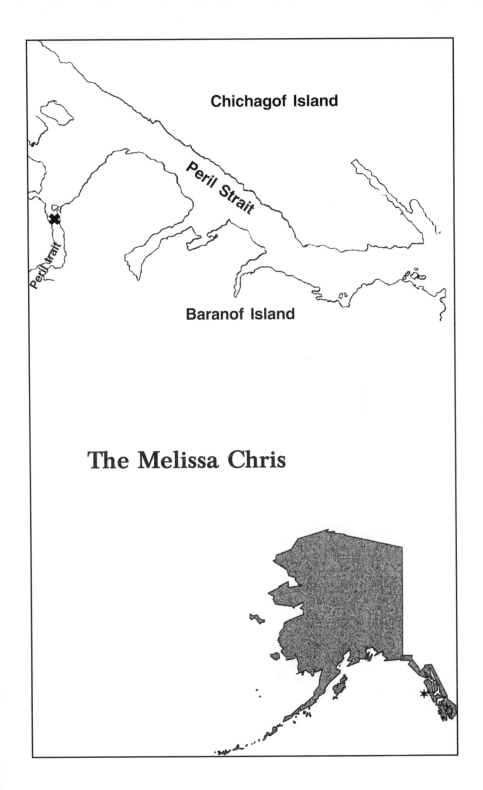

Chichagof Island

Peril Strait

Peril Strait

Baranof Island

The Melissa Chris

A Summer on the Mellissa Chris

By Randy Berg as told to Wilma Williams

It was 1988. After spending my summers in Alaska for the last ten years, my high school buddy, Rich Gindhart, and I decided to start a small brine refrigeration business in Bellingham, Washington. One of the first contracts we had was to repair the brine system on the 90-foot tender, *Mellissa Chris,* and install a second one.

While we were doing this job, Marvin Hansen, the skipper, asked, "How would you boys like to go to Alaska with me this summer if the contract comes through with Peter Pan in King Cove?"

Marvin was a rather husky individual with many years of experience in Alaskan waters. I had spent the last ten summers on various boats going north, but, besides the fact that we had started this little business, this boat had a reputation for sinking. It had done it twice before. Rumor had it that on one of these occasions the keel had actually been broken and never properly repaired, causing it to handle badly. Also it was in dire need of repair.

After summing up all of the negative factors, we didn't hesitate to say, "No, we don't think so. There are a lot of things that need fixing on this boat before it should go to sea."

That, however, did not close the issue. Captain Hansen, no doubt, liked the idea of having built-in help with the brine systems and kept improving the picture.

"How about, if we bring the boat up to par and you boys can do your refrigeration business when we are in port. Most of the boats that need refrigeration repair will be up north for the summer, and you should make pretty good money."

We were weakening. This might not be a bad idea after all. In the end we agreed to go and were hired immediately to start on the repairs. The skipper even allowed us to contact a friend, John Jones, to come aboard as cook.

The boat was in very bad shape, and the owners resisted putting the necessary funds into repairing it, so we did a lot of makeshift repairs. We worked from the day we were hired, all the way on the trip north, and until the night before the first opening, trying to get the main problems solved.

Northbound, we were blessed with good weather. That is, up until the last night out. The storm came up quickly. The light went out in the engine room, and in the dark room, while replacing the bulb, I was a bit unnerved to see tiny threads of light showing through the upper part of the hull. The working of the boat in the storm put two feet of water in the bilge.

"There seems to be a lot of water coming in," I reported to the skipper.

"What's the big deal?" the skipper scoffed. " All boats leak."

Well, I guess so, but that was more leak than I liked.

"But, skipper, that is with all of the pumps going full

bore." From that day on, the two-inch pump ran full bore, day and night.

The next serious storm hit about midway through the season. We were headed for the cannery with a full load of fish when it came up. We had two other pumps and I got them all going, but from the beginning of the storm, Rich and I fought to keep all of them going. The boat was taking a hellish beating, and, personally, I thought it was about as bad as it could get. Wrong! Suddenly we were into a huge ocean tide rip. The water seemed to come at us from all directions. Then a side stay snapped and all hell broke loose. The main boom and both cargo booms started swinging wildly as the boat rolled and pitched uncontrollably one way and then the other.

Rich and I got the hydraulic motor running and lowered all of the booms to the deck.

With the booms on the deck, we started trying to figure out how to get a line on them, to tie them down. All the while, they whipped back and forth, tearing away everything in their path. About that time we broke free of the tide rip and managed to get the booms secured to the deck cleats. For the first time since the storm began, we had time to look around us. The side of the wheelhouse was bashed in. Broken glass was strewn around with splintered pieces of wood. Nothing, absolutely nothing, had escaped the battering. It truly looked like we had been under siege by an enemy using cannons.

Once we got to port, John Jones, our cook, showed very good sense and left for home. Rich and I still felt we should see the season through.

In late August, we went to Prince William Sound to haul a few loads of pinks from the hatchery to the cannery in Valdez then start our homeward journey. When we were actually on our way home, I breathed a sigh of relief with every southbound mile. It was hard to believe our good luck at still being alive and afloat. Down through White Stone Pass and Hoonah Strait, that 16-71 Jimmy diesel screamed like a banshee as she pushed us homeward.

The weather was good, and the skipper was on the wheel

coming through Peril Straits. Rick and I were in our bunks sleeping a very relaxed sleep. Everything was great and we were headed home. Suddenly, we came to a screeching, grinding halt that very nearly threw us onto the floor. Running up on deck, we found that we were hard aground on a reef and listing hard over on the starboard side. The skipper shouted, "Turn off the engine!" I opened the door to the engine room to follow his instructions, only to find it was already filled with water. So much for that idea.

Rich was pulling the life raft down off the top of the wheelhouse, and I gave him a hand. It inflated easily, but we were soon aware that it had been a mistake to inflate it before we got it into the water. Tugging and swearing, we finally got it into the water, and the skipper got in.

The beach was really quite close to land, but two brown bears paced back and forth on the rocky beach, pausing now and then to look our way. I thought they were perhaps saying, in bear language, "I'll take the one with the blue hat. He looks delicious." "Okay, but let's wait and see if they come ashore and save us the swim."

Since the radio was still above water, Rich climbed in to give the Coast Guard a call. Their answer came crackling back, "I'm sorry but this is apparently not a life-threatening situation. There are other boats in the area that can be of assistance." I glanced dubiously at the bears on the beach and hoped the "not life threatening" part was true.

Rich was waist deep in cold water when he suddenly let out a yelp. "What the heck?" he shouted. "You aren't going to believe this." He was wrong about that. At this point I would have believed about anything. "There is a fish swimming around here in the cabin."

Nearly five hours went by before we heard the gentle thump of a diesel engine across the quiet waters. All eyes scanned the horizon for the source of the sound. When it came closer we could see it was the *Star of the North*, a tour boat out of Sitka. Although they didn't take us aboard they gave us hot coffee and advised us that the *St. Lazaria* was right behind them and would take us into port.

In a few hours we were in port and the harrowing summer was at last at an end, and we were certainly glad of that.

Epilogue:

Randy Berg decided after that interesting summer there must be a safer way to make a living and has been working construction in the Bellingham, Washington area since then. Rich Gindhart was unavailable for comment but is still following the sea. Randy did not know what had happened to the skipper through the years. And what of the boat that lay gasping on the reef? It was taken from its rocky resting place and plies the waters of southeastern Alaska as a longliner. She was given a new name, which must have helped because she hasn't sunk in quite awhile.

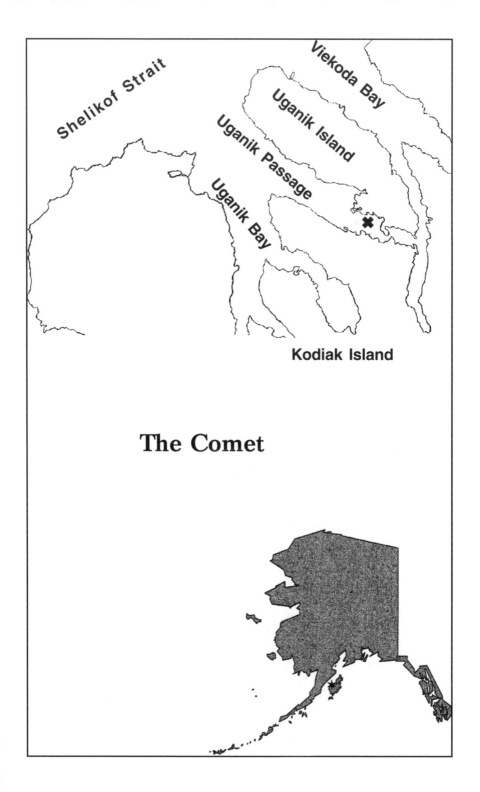

Shelikof Strait

Viekoda Bay

Uganik Island

Uganik Passage

Uganik Bay

Kodiak Island

The Comet

The Comet's Last Haul

By Lola Harvey, as told to Wilma Williams

Comet

Around 10 a.m. on a sunny morning in the latter part of August 1959, I donned my oldest slacks and a blouse that I had been looking for a good excuse to throw away, and attacked the project of painting the outside of my house. I left the windows open closest to where I was painting, in order to hear any incoming calls on the radio that were my responsibility in our Harvey Flying Service business.

I looked over the freshly painted wall carefully to see if there were any places I had missed. Satisfied that all was as it should be, I climbed down to move the ladder, in the process glancing out over the channel that flowed by my Kodiak home.

From years of watching the boats come and go, I recognized Al Owens' boat, the *Comet*. She was riding low in the water, with a bundle of lumber on deck and, of course, the ever-faithful skiff on top of it. "Now, what on earth are the Owenses doing with all that lumber on board," I wondered. "Of course. That is to build the house at their fishing sites in Uganik Bay for their daughter, Deedie, and her husband." I remembered them talking about doing that.

They were personal friends, and when I saw Al and Hazel waving, I waved back before resetting my ladder. Looking back, I noticed Deedie on deck. Probably her husband, Wayne, and brother, Bob, were aboard too, but I didn't see them. From years of living with the tides, I glanced at my watch. It seemed they were later than they usually were on the tide for that run.

The day wore on, and I temporarily gave up on the painting project as the radio calls became more frequent. A couple of hours had gone by.

On the boat, Al was on the wheel. Hazel and Deedie fixed coffee and chatted amiably, while Wayne and Bob puttered and talked about the upcoming project. The wind was not too bad until they came out of Kupreanof Strait. A northwest wind was really kicking up, and Al didn't like that with the load he had on.

Wanting to take no chances, he turned the boat down Viekoda Bay to stay out of the weather. Shortly after coming into Uganik Passage, there was a sudden thunk and a lurch. It only took moments for Al to see the water coming into the engine room of the boat. There would be no getting off this rock. It was jammed clear through the stern of the boat, while the bow rose and fell on the choppy water. Al called the Coast Guard, but was unable to get an answer. He turned his radio to 2512, where he would try to get Harvey Flying Service.

The radio came alive with Al's calm voice. "KXK 28, KXK 28, this is the *Comet* calling."

"*Comet*, KXK 28. Go ahead, Al," I answered.

"Lola, I was wondering if you could give Bill a call and see if he could come out to Uganik Passage."

"All right, Al. Is this for a passenger?" I asked.

"Well, yes. We are on Senator Rock in the passage here, and we are sinking. I tried to call the Coast Guard, but can't seem to raise them. Be sure and tell him that it is blowing northeasterly and there is a pretty good chop here."

Now, that is the sort of call that gets your attention right away. "Al, I will call him. Please stand by."

"That's a roger," Al came back, and then added with his dry sense of humor, "I really don't think I will be going any-where."

Out on the boat, Al turned from the radio. Everyone was waiting to see what the next move would be. There wasn't any panic, just a sad feeling of losing a boat that had been home and transportation for them for a very long time. It had been a cannery tender before it was theirs and had a long record of faithful service. Below deck, the big old Atlas engine purred away as if it was determined to do its best till the end.

"I guess I better go shut the engine down," Al said. His voice was sad. Deedie listened to the purring sound, hoping she would hear that comforting sound again, but that was not to be.

I called my husband at the hangar office and gave him the message, also mentioning that the *Comet* had all the mate-rial for a 28-by-28 house on board. Bill was as calm as Al when he said, "Tell Al I'm leaving now with the Pacer on floats and to hang on. The swimming in that area is lousy."

I relayed the message to Al, and his voice sounded re-lieved when he answered back.

I heard Bill call Leonard Helgason and Fred Sullivan at their bear camp in Terror Bay, asking if they could come over and give a hand. Might be able to save some of the building materials. Good idea.

Later, when I heard Bill call the *Comet*, I was surprised to hear Hazel's frightened voice on the radio, saying, "Bill, where are you?" With Hazel's attitude toward radios, I wasn't sure whether she was more frightened of the radio or their present situation.

"I'm right over your head," Bill answered.

"Oh, there you are. You were coming in so loud, but I couldn't see you."

"Hazel, tell Al that I am going to have to land over between the islands to get on the water."

Al's voice came on the radio. "Bill, Bob and Wayne are getting the skiff ready to take the women over to the island where you are going to land. Better not try to come out here. OK?"

Once the matter was settled, the radio was quiet, and I wondered how things were going. I knew I would have to wait to hear the rest of the story.

When Bill got home I was so happy to hear that all of the news was good. He had to take the women, one at a time, on over to their place at Mush Bay, as it was too rough to try a takeoff with both of them in the plane.

The two men arrived from Terror Bay with a boat, and, outside of the soggy ceiling tile, all the building material was salvaged. There were some wrinkles and fat spots in the chip board that ended up on the cabin walls, a reminder of the harrowing experience. As the tide went out, the men were able to get some of the personal items from inside the boat.

In Mush Bay, it was three days before Hazel and Deedie

knew the final outcome, when the men finally arrived there.

When the tide came back in, the *Comet* sank beneath the waves forever, leaving only the tip of the mast showing above the waves.

Epilogue:

I want to thank Bill and Lola's daughter, Louise, for first telling me the story of her dad rescuing these people, Lola for giving me more details, and Deedie for her personal input that helped to flesh out the story. Bill Harvey, Al and Hazel Owens have all passed away. Deedie and Lola still live in Kodiak. Deedie still fishes, and Lola is busy driving tour bus and writing.

Index

Maxwell, Tommy 55
Mellissa Chris 110
Mia Dawn 23
Minix, Mike 101
Miss Heidi Maru 55
Miss Lisa 61
Morgan, Tom 12

N

Neimiroff, Marty 26
Nelson, George 80
Ng, Jimmy 26

O

Openheim, Craig 34
Orth, Michael 9
Owens, Al 117

P

Payne, Mrs. 80
Prince, Jack 9

R

Reynolds, Rich 18

S

Sally J 34
Sand Piper 93
Shears, Sharon 9
Sheldon, Rick 68
Shelford, Lee 45
Sirius 9
Stall, Hugo 41
Sullivan, Fred 118

T

Tabhone, Carlton 101
Tempest 45
Thompson, Fred 9
Trakowski, Tiny 84
Trondsen, Chris 78
Troxell, Nick 34

V

Vargus, David 56
Vaughn, Jackie 42

W

West, Chuck 68
Williams, Charlie 93
Wilson, Darryl 24

Y

Yukon 78

Wilma Williams was born in Washington state, but came to Alaska with her parents at the age of eight months and has spent most of her life in the state. Taking her children along, she salmon fished commercially in Bristol Bay and operated the Coffee Point boat storage until 1990, when she retired. Since that time, she has been writing and enjoying her home in Homer, Alaska.

Rhonda Shelford Jansen was born in Alaska, and it was her home for the first 14 years of her life. After living in Homer, Kodiak and Dutch Harbor, she studied art at the University of Washington in Seattle. She now lives in Mukilteo, just north of Seattle, with her commercial fisherman husband, Dan, and their three children. Her art work specializes in boats.

Other Books by Wilma Williams

If You've Got it to Do, a love story between a teenager
who did not want to come here and the state of Alaska.
Life, livin' and lovin' in Alaska, from 1926 on. $15.95

This is Coffee Point: Go Ahead; *A Mother's Story of Fishing
& Survival at Alaska's Bristol Bay.* A mother relives the
beauty and dangers of fishing remote Alaska beach sites
with her children. $15.95.

Order Blank

Please send me the following books:

_____ *If You've Got it to Do* @ $15.95 each $_____
_____ *This is Coffee Point...* @ $15.95 each $_____
_____ *Alaska Sea Escapes* @ $14.95 each $_____
Postage & handling ($2/book regular
    mail or $4/book priority) $_____
Total Enclosed $_____

Send to:_____

_____

_____

Wizard Works, P.O. Box 1125, Homer, AK 99603

Order Blank

Please send me the following books:

_____ *If You've Got it to Do* @ $15.95 each $_____
_____ *This is Coffee Point...* @ $15.95 each $_____
_____ *Alaska Sea Escapes* @ $14.95 each $_____
Postage & handling ($2/book regular
    mail or $4/book priority) $_____
Total Enclosed $_____

Send to:_____

_____

_____

Wizard Works, P.O. Box 1125, Homer, AK 99603